IT'S THE LAW!

IT'S THE LAW!

A Young Person's Guide
to Our Legal System

Annette Carrel

VOLCANO
· PRESS ·

Volcano, California

Library of Congress Cataloging-in-Publication Data

Carrel, Annette.
    It's the law : a young person's guide to our legal
system / by Annette Carrel.
        p.   cm.
    Includes index.
    ISBN 1-884244-01-7
    1. Law—United States—Juvenile literature.
2. Criminal justice, Administration of—United
States—Juvenile literature.   3. United States—
Constitutional law—Juvenile literature.   [1. Law.
2. Criminal justice, Administration of.]   I. Title.
KF387.C34   1994
349.73—dc20
[347.3]   94-13552
                              CIP
                              AC

Cover art by Wayne Quinn, reprinted with permission.
A fee has been donated to the Elizabeth Taylor AIDS
Foundation in consideration of the owner of the art.

Design/Production: David Charlsen
Editorial: Zoe Brown
Typesetting: ImageComp

Please enclose $12.95 for each copy of **IT'S THE LAW!**
ordered. For postage and handling, add $4.50 for the
first book and $1.00 for each additional book. California
residents only add appropriate sales tax. Contact
Volcano Press for quantity discount rates and for a free
current catalog.
   Volcano Press, Inc., P.O. Box 270, Volcano CA 95689
       (209) 296-3445   FAX: (209) 296-4515

Printed in the United States of America.

Contents

This book is dedicated to

ROSE AND LOUIS
for life

BOB
for love

LAURA, DAVID AND JASON
for the exquisite joy of being your mother

Acknowledgments

There are many people I would like to thank or acknowledge. The list includes James Carroll Sr., member of the Marin County Board of Education, who extended his love of language to my manuscript which he corrected with care and patience.

James Carroll Jr., officer with the City of Concord Police Department, and Frances Stecker, sergeant with the Santa Barbara Marshal's Office, who checked and rechecked my material for accuracy.

Don Sweeney, my friend and attorney, for his sage advice.

And our wonderful judges, court clerks, bailiffs, and other court attachés of the Santa Barbara Superior and Municipal Courts who are always willing to answer questions, share space, and tolerate my invasions with large classes of students. They indeed live up to the ideals within our justice system with their fine spirit and high level of performance.

Chapter 1
WHAT THIS BOOK IS ABOUT

This book is about law and the code of laws that govern what you do. It is also about what happens if you break the law. This is a book for young people, boys and girls, young men and young women, just like you.

As long as you must obey laws—and someday you will be making laws yourself—it is a good thing to know what this "law business" is all about.

> "Put your hands in the air! Place them on this wall. Keep your hands there and take two steps back. Spread your legs. You are under arrest!" By now you should be pretty uncomfortable! The officer will search you for weapons and then apply the handcuff to one arm behind your back. Next he or she will apply the other handcuff. You are standing with your head against the wall, with your hands behind your back, and your legs spread. This means that you will not be able to move without falling. It also means that the officer has subdued you, and you are under arrest.
>
> What happens to you now? What can you do about it? Do you have any rights?
>
> The laws that could help you should interest you now more than any other time of your life. This is the big time. This is real. No one is pretending or playing. The

officer has observed you breaking the law—or has other
good reason for believing you did. You are under arrest. If
you have been arrested on the same charge before, you
can be charged with a felony. If you are convicted of a
felony, most likely you will go to jail or prison.

Later in this book, you'll learn exactly what happens when
people get into trouble with the law. But first of all, we'll need
to think about what the law is.

The laws that govern your world are mostly invisible. They
control much of what goes on around you without your even
being aware of them. You are apt to learn about a law only if it
gets in the way of something you want to do—or if someone
breaks the law and harms you.

If you were born in this country, you began right away as
part of our legal-justice system. Your birth was legally registered on a birth certificate. The doctor or midwife who delivered you had a legal permit (license) to do so. If you were
born in a hospital, you may be sure it had a legal charter for
which it had to qualify in order to be in business. The medicines they gave you came from a legal laboratory which had
to maintain certain standards. These medicines had to be approved by the Food and Drug Administration before they
could be used on people. I could go on, and on, and on. Even
if you were born in another country, the laws of this land
protect you when you are here.

We have a justice system in the United States that involves
the entire country and includes federal law and federal
courts. Each state also has its own justice system with state
laws and state courts. Both systems are guided by the Constitution of the United States and, in addition, each state also has
its own State Constitution. Each state has the right to make
and enforce its own laws *provided they do not conflict* with
federal laws or the U. S. Constitution. Most of the information
in this book is essentially true of all the states, but some
actions can be legal in some states and not legal in others. What
is allowed in one state might not be allowed in another. If you

commit robbery in California you might be punished differently than you would for the same offense in Mississippi. A picture or a song recording might be considered outrageous and banned in one state, but praised for artistic value in another state. You can check with your own local justice system, perhaps your own district attorney, if you are particularly interested in whether a certain law is the same where you live.

As you read this book you will find mentions of the civil rights guaranteed by the U. S. Constitution and its amendments. To understand these statements, you should know that the Constitution is the plan of government that was written by the founders of our country. The amendments are additions to the Constitution. We call the first ten amendments the *Bill of Rights,* which protects us from unjust and unreasonable actions of the police, the legal system, and other parts of the government. Laws in this country must follow the ideas in the Constitution and the amendments. (Further on in this book, Chapters 16 and 17 explain the Constitution in more detail.)

Law is in many ways an adult subject. It involves serious business. It deals with life and death, with freedom and the loss of freedom, and with business. Law has become a popular subject on television shows and movies. You probably know more about it than you think you do. I hope this book will help you sort out some of your ideas, some of the things you have heard and seen but not understood. Let's hope, too, that it will awaken your interest in the law, our government, and your role in this important and exciting area of your life.

Chapter 2
WHAT IS A LAW?

Law! What does the word mean? Let's start with a formal answer which is full of big words, and then we'll look at what they mean. Remember, we are talking about the laws of our country.

> A law is a rule which modifies behavior and is adopted by people through their legislators, which will govern the actions of the affected populace (those people who are directly concerned) for a desired order which will protect the people and allow them to enjoy the freedoms and justice guaranteed by the Constitution.

This is a lot of words! But if you read carefully, a phrase at a time, they will soon make sense. These laws govern our behavior and tell us what we may and may not do. And these laws are made by people like you and me. Before I let other people tell ME what to do—bossing ME around, I want to know what this law business is all about, and I hope you do too. A simpler definition of the law is:

> A set of enforced rules under which a society is governed.

Law sets up rules that define a person's rights and obligations. This word *obligation* is very important and a word that people often do not think about. They shout and demand their rights, but seldom realize that this system of government can work only if everyone participates, if everyone accepts his or her responsibility to live lawfully within this system of government. For someone who does not accept this obligation, the law sets penalties and states how the government will enforce the rules.

The word *law* generally refers to a rule established by a government and enforced by some law-keeping agency such as the police, sheriff, or marshal's office.

Rules that are not set up by the government are quite different. They are enforceable only within the area in which the rule was made, such as a gymnasium, a school, or a work place. If you do not obey a rule, you can be thrown out of the gym, expelled from school, or fired from the job; but you cannot be arrested *unless that rule is also against the law.*

People study law to learn about legal rules, but that is not what this book is about. You'd probably find it pretty boring to just read hundreds of legal rules, and even then we couldn't say that you know all about law. But we will have an easier time obeying laws if we understand more about them. Since we live in a complicated, crowded society, we have to be aware of how our actions affect others. Let's start by talking about this in a "real-life" way, a way that may make it easier to understand this law business.

Foundations of American Law

When early settlers landed in America some time after Columbus, there were not very many people there. The first settlers spread out and started homes, farms, and businesses. Some chose good land to farm. Others found groves of trees and started lumber businesses. Still others built mills and churches and schools.

Things went very well at first. There was plenty of land and not many people. Little towns were formed in many areas. After a while, however, more and more people came who were also looking for a better life. As the little towns became more populated, people started to get in each others' way. Some built on property belonging to others. Many people started businesses in competition with other businesses. Some felt the newcomers shouldn't be allowed to do this, and they wanted laws to protect what they considered to be their rights.

When the English settlers came to North America, they brought English common law as their guide to setting up rules for living in this new land.

> Common law is not written in statutes or codes. It is developed over time by judicial decisions based on custom and precedent.

Since the beginning of our nation, common law has been the basis for most American law. In states such as California and Texas, however, there are still some laws based on Spanish laws. The State Constitution of Louisiana shows the influence of the French and Spanish legal systems. Some of the laws in Louisiana are based on the Napoleonic Code.

The Law and Your Rights

Let's get back to that word *law* and another word that is used so much now, the word *rights*. When we think of the word *law*, we may think of all those words that tell what we can and cannot do. Words that boss us around. Words like, "Keep Out," "No Trespassing," "Keep Off," "Thou Shalt Not . . ." All of this is very negative. Don't! Do not! No! But the real meaning of law is not negative at all. Law is an enabler! It makes us able. It allows us to be free to do things.

Think for a minute. Suppose you get a wonderful idea and you invent something. Now, if you show your invention to someone else, he might copy it and could sell your idea as if it were his own. But because we have a law that protects you, you can make sure you have all the rights to your invention. You do this by taking out a patent. A patent assures that you, the inventor, are the only one who can sell or use your idea. That is one example of a law "giving" you freedom.

Here is another example. Suppose you write a book or a poem, or music; or suppose you work for a computer company and you produce a new computer game like Nintendo, and you want to share it with others. What will stop them from copying it and taking credit for writing it? Again there is a law to protect you. If you get your work copyrighted, no one can legally use it without giving you credit. You are the only one that can collect payment for selling it. Again, you are given freedom by the law. If you look on the back of the title-page in this book, you will find the word and symbol "Copyright ©." This will protect me, Annette Carrel, from other people who might want to use my words.

How about building a home on your land? Suppose your house was finished and someone said that you built it on his land? What could you do? Of course you could threaten him with violence, but then again he could do the same to you. That is a bad solution. But there is a legal way to protect yourself ahead of time. You can get a deed for your property. That way, if you and the other person want to settle the matter legally, you have proof of your ownership.

We could go on and on with examples. I hope you are beginning to think of other laws that help you. What all this means is that law is an enabler. Without laws we would be afraid to leave our homes, or share our ideas, or join each other as partners.

Two Other Important Ideas

We'll go into more detail about why we need laws, how we got them, who made them, and what we can do about them, starting with Chapter 5. But first, let's consider a couple of very important ideas that have a lot to do with the law: justice, and control.

Chapter 3
JUSTICE

Justice means that every man must receive
what is due him,
love means that every man should receive
the consideration and compassion he needs,
taken together, a nation must rule in a manner
mindful of the dignity and worth of each individual . . .
and for the common good.
Can the ideals of justice and love be accomplished
by laws?

Adapted from Your Laws
by Frank K. Kelly

As we discuss law, we must also consider justice, for law is based on ideas of justice.

I pledge allegiance to the Flag of the United States of America, and to the Republic for which it stands, one Nation under God, indivisible, with liberty and justice for all.

That word *justice* is not very large, yet it stands for one of the most valuable gifts you possess. Justice is not something you can hold in your hand. It is a concept, an idea. It is worth more money than you can ever think of. It is why most people

8

left their homelands and emigrated to America. It is why we sometimes fought wars; it is why many other nations look to the United States as a leader in the world.

Justice is easy to spell. It is also easy to define. Stop for a minute and try to think of all the words that describe justice. There are a lot of them, aren't there? But the best is just the simple word, *fair*. And *fair* means that we must accept that you and I, and all other people, have "equal rights"—and equal responsibility!

When we pledge to the flag, we speak of liberty and justice—these are ideals. Liberty and justice are the wonderful guarantees on which our government is based. And remember the phrase, *for all*.

To insure liberty and justice we have established a government of the people, by the people, and for the people. *The people* means all people—not just certain people. All people, rich and poor, young and old, smart and not smart, important and famous people, and ordinary people. It means that we have to think of others besides ourselves if we are to live well within our justice system.

When the new nation began with the Declaration of Independence, which declared all men equal, this equality was acknowledged as a God-given right, not a right that men could give and take away. The early leaders of this new free country formed the new government within a Constitution which established these rights. All our laws developed since that time are based on that simple word *justice*.

The ideals of justice can go beyond what is merely a legal right. To do this we must also consider the ideals of love and an expanded idea of caring. This chapter started by asking you if these ideals could be combined with the ideals of justice and be accomplished by laws. I think the answer is, "Yes." We have many, many laws that protect the disabled, the weak, the young, the powerless; and we are constantly creating more. For example, laws now require ramps to enable people in wheelchairs to use the streets and enter public buildings. It would be an ideal world if the dignity and the worth of individuals could be respected without laws; but as a society we haven't come that far yet. Laws remind us of our obligations and allow us to reach for ideals. Since WE are the lawmakers, there are no limits to the good we can do.

Chapter 4
CONTROL

The other day as I was walking through the courthouse, I saw a deputy walking three prisoners to their courtrooms. One man had handcuffs attached to a chain around his waist. He also had ankle-irons, which limited the way he could walk. The second man was in handcuffs and walked normally. The third man just walked along with the guard. All three men were in prison clothing so I knew they had come from the jail to appear in court.

Now, I was seeing three different levels of control. The man heavily chained and cuffed was indeed a threat to "the people" and probably to himself. The second man was treated with a level of control that reflected his ability to control himself, and the third man was expected to behave within his own control system—that means he was expected to act as a normal person would.

Most people don't like others to tell them what they can or cannot do. They feel they can take care of themselves. That is certainly the best way to live. That means policing yourself, having self-control. It means adjusting your sense of freedom to consider the rights of others. It means being responsible for your actions. We need laws and the people to enforce laws only when persons do not respect the rights of others.

Think about it this way. When you walk down the street and see a police car, are you filled with fear? Probably not unless you are doing something wrong. Only if you had committed a crime, or were doing something reckless, or were where you were not supposed to be, then the sight of a police officer might worry you.

If I am driving and a police car comes up behind me, I check to see if I am driving correctly and then relax. I just want to make sure the officer is not trying to pass me on the way to an emergency. If I see the police car's lights blinking, I move out of the way. I am in control of my actions.

Let's imagine driving without the white line painted down the middle of the street. Imagine no traffic lanes, no traffic signs or traffic lights. Imagine no speed limit. Wow! Do you think people would drive as we do now? Would they take turns crossing the street? Most people would, I think. Most of us are comfortable with a system. But there are those people who only think: I, mine, me! me! ME!

Some of you are too young to drive right now, but you will be old enough soon. Let's talk about your world, and the controls in your world. If your parents never told you when to go to bed, I wonder when you would do so. If your teachers never gave directions, do you think everyone would walk instead of running in the halls? If you could talk whenever you wanted in school, would everyone be considerate and not disturb the rest of the class? What would the play yard be like? What do you think a football game would be like without rules and referees? The game would probably seem like a wrestling match with the players all over each other.

For some people controls are not a problem. They would be fair and considerate with or without rules or laws. Other persons only think of themselves and what they want right now. They never think back to realize what a mess they made by their actions. They always want to be first in line. They always take the most. They push and bully to get whatever they want. And so, as a society of all the people, we must take control of them.

We make rules and decide punishments. Be aware that I am saying *we*. That means you and me. So many people think the law is "way over there," and that it belongs to other people way over there, "outside somewhere." No, no! The law is here where we are. It is us! You and I. And the law will only be as good as the people participating in it.

Chapter 5
WHY DO WE NEED LAWS?

Do you think most people would drive over a bridge,
like the Golden Gate Bridge or the Brooklyn Bridge, if
that bridge didn't have any side rails? The road is wide
enough, and the lanes have painted lines. But if there
were no rails—just the water far below—we would be
terrified. That is how most of us would feel if we did not
have any laws in our world.

From earliest history, wherever people lived together, they
found it necessary to make rules of conduct to settle disputes,
and rules for the organization of their government. Many big
words again—but stay with me. I'll give you an example based
on your own space and your own rights.

Think about the average school yard at lunch time. If a
teacher kept most of the school in and sent just two students
out to play, each with his or her own ball to play with, do you
think the teacher would need to make many rules for those
two to follow? No, probably not. That situation is quite simple.

Now think about that same school yard at lunch time when
the whole school is out to play! The space is crowded. Everyone wants to do what he or she wants. Now you need many
rules. Rules about what you can and cannot do, rules about
not running in the walkways, rules about noise, about safety,

about courtesy, rules about cleaning up, about not interfering with others, and on and on.

At school, when one group or one student interferes with the rights of others, what is your solution? If you choose to fight it out, the largest or the strongest person—or the biggest group or gang—will usually win. But remember that there is often someone larger or stronger than you, or bigger than your gang. You can't count on winning that kind of fight. So most often you would go to someone in charge to ask for a fair solution. You want someone who will be fair to make decisions.

The same is true of the adult world. Most people do not want to fight with others. Most would rather go before a judge to get a legal decision. This is a form of fighting with words and brains, rather than fighting with fists or weapons. A judge has sworn to be fair and to uphold the law. Of course, we often read about someone shooting or beating someone else because of an argument. Most of the time both people are the losers, and the only thing they end with is heartache and sorrow.

Chapter 6
WHO MAKES OUR LAWS?

Hey! Vote for me! I am going to do what you want—no more school, no more homework, no more going to the doctor and getting those nasty old shots. No more vegetables—only cookies and ice cream. Vote for me! All those other guys are no good. It is your right to have everything the way you want it, and I am going to make many laws that will change things.

It sounds like election time again, with the candidates promising anything and everything to get votes. Newspapers and television carry many messages to the voter. Candidates pay thousands of dollars for these ads and commercials. You are smart enough not to vote for the person who would promise all the things above. But suppose others are not as wise, and they vote him or her into office? Can such a person change all our laws and make many new ones, just like that? It is not that easy, thank heavens. Read on.

Deciding Who Should
Make the Laws

The men who created our Constitution established three branches of government, which would share the authority and power among many people instead of a king or a royal group.

In the lands the early settlers left behind there were different systems for deciding who would rule or govern. Most of those countries had royalty—people who were called kings and queens, or perhaps they were czars or emperors or mikados, and everyone had to bow to them, to do what they said. Other lawmakers were noblemen or persons who were considered to be of a special "upper class." They were called lords or chiefs or shoguns, or any other name that gave them power.

When a baby was born it belonged to a class, and it didn't matter how that baby grew, how smart that baby was, or how hard that person worked when grown, he or she could never change classes. A person born into the "lower class" might have little or no choice about what work to do or where to live. The lower-class person had to obey those "above." He had to obey the powerful person who owned the land, and who, in many ways, owned him. This was just fine if you were one of the lucky ones and had all the wealth and power. But the people who were part of the lower class, the "working class," had few rights. Laws were made by the nobles—the upper class—and of course the laws favored the nobility.

When people came to this new land called America, they wanted a form of government that would treat all persons equally, a government that would give all people an equal chance to improve their way of life. They had given up whatever they owned in their homeland; they left people they knew and loved, so they could live under a system that insured freedom. It must have been a difficult and frightening decision to make that move.

The early settlers chose some very talented and learned men to lead them to a new way of government. Some of these men came from the so-called upper class, but they all believed strongly that government should be just and based on every person's rights. Of course, laws were needed to insure these rights.

It was very important to design a government that shared the power among the people. Like the trunk of a tree, our government has a strong central ideal or force based on the Constitution. The power to make it work is divided among three separate groups, or *branches*—the legislative (law-making), the executive (enforcing the law), and the judicial (insuring that all laws and actions conform to the rights and limits within the Constitution).

The legislative was the first branch established. To legislate is to make or pass laws. The legislature is a group of citizens with the power to make laws. In those early days the legislature met to design laws that would guide each individual's behavior for the best interest of all the people. They remembered that in the countries they left, only the royalty or very important people made laws.

So the creators of the Constitution formed a government of, by, and for the people. The legislative branch was divided into two groups of people, the House of Representatives and the Senate. Together these two groups are called the Congress. Members of the House of Representatives are called representatives or congressmen and congresswomen. Members of the Senate are called senators. These legislators are ordinary people elected by voters to act for them.

Choosing the Lawmakers

It is important to take time to talk about that word *elected*. It means that the men and women now in Congress were voted into their jobs by your parents and neighbors and—by me. You may vote when you reach the age of eighteen. (Sometimes a member of Congress is appointed instead of being elected. This only happens under special circumstances, such as the death of another member.)

Your members of Congress do the talking for you. They take your ideas to the Congress. It is very important for you to know what they think, to know what they do and what they promise to do for you. It is your responsibility to know for whom you are voting. And it is also your responsibility to tell these lawmakers what *you* think and what *you* want them to do, for *you are the government!*

Earlier I said that justice means every person should receive what is due him or her. I said that love means that all persons should receive the consideration and compassion they need. I then asked: can these two ideals be accomplished through laws? I certainly hope so! Remember who makes these laws. Who shapes laws, revises or repeals the laws—holds them wonderfully high or lowers them shamefully? Remember who chooses these lawmakers? And remember:

> The effectiveness of laws depends on the people's willingness to accept them and obey them.

Every Citizen Is Responsible for Government

We already talked about the political commercials or ads all over the newspapers and on television before an election. There are constant speeches full of promises by the candidates, hoping that they will say something the voters want to hear. They want your vote! They realize how important you are! Everyone over the age of eighteen who registers to vote is allowed to go to the polls at election time and cast his or her one vote. In order to get elected, that candidate must have the votes of people like you. Do not give your vote away without thinking. You are very special, and powerful. Get involved!

Now, even though I get to vote my one vote, I also care how others cast their votes. I might want to work for a certain candidate or for a special cause. Most candidates have campaign offices where there are many jobs for volunteers. You do not have to be eighteen years old to help in election campaigns. Some of these jobs might be to phone voters, to help mail campaign literature, to place posters around town, to arrange meetings for the candidate, to ask for money to help pay some of the huge cost of a campaign.

Some laws, called "initiatives" or "propositions," are decided directly by the voters instead of in the legislature. If you are supporting an "issue," a special interest of yours, you might want to campaign for the passage of the proposition on the ballot. Maybe you are interested in ecology, and someone has proposed a law to help stop pollution. You might work very hard to get information to voters so they become aware of this issue.

Suppose there was a candidate who is proposing a new law that would make all school students attend classes from eight in the morning until six o'clock in the evening. And suppose you heard that this candidate also wanted to have school on Saturdays and Sundays, and that all children should do six hours of homework every day. Would you want to vote for that person or for that proposition? Maybe you merely heard about this candidate from a friend. You would probably want to see and hear the candidate yourself on television or at a meeting.

How about that candidate who was calling for your vote at the very beginning of this chapter? This candidate seemed to think schools are dumb and they cost too much money, and students don't like them anyway—and kids should just be free to lie around if they want to. Suppose he or she also promised that children would never have to go to the doctor and get shots because they hurt a tiny bit? Would you vote for that person? At least I am sure you would want to take a good look at that candidate and maybe ask a few important questions.

I was being a bit silly in making my point. But people are willing to hear and read about the persons who want to become lawmakers. They pay taxes and own businesses. They may care about the environment, or want peace, or want their tax money spent a certain way. They want to know the candidate they vote for.

A lawmaker who would make such silly promises would have a surprise coming. It is not an easy matter to make or change laws. Read on.

Chapter 7
HOW OUR LAWS ARE MADE

Recently the nation was warned that a computer virus was going to strike at a certain time and might destroy the memory on millions of computers. This could mean millions and millions of dollars to companies that would lose time and their ability to conduct business. Such an act would amount to stealing, to an invasion of privacy, to destroying property, to committing vandalism.

The computer world is rather new. Thirty years ago very few people had computers, and few businesses were literally "run" by them. But these days, if computers break down, the affairs of many businesses stop. Just watch what happens at the airport when their computers break down. It is a mess.

Sometimes New Laws
Are Needed

When something useful is invented or developed to be shared among the people, there is always a chance that someone can or will abuse the rights of others. To make sure that this is not done, certain regulations or rules or laws are needed. The need is usually determined when an abuse happens.

Computer crime is new, and computer laws are new and not well-written. We are not even aware of the next computer crimes that will be invented. Many high-tech companies have special security divisions to detect viruses. Lawmakers are going to be very busy making new laws for this new field.

> We determine what is moral and legal.
> Our thinking shapes the laws.
> Do our laws shape our thinking?

We Americans have the right to decide about the laws under which we live, the rules laid down by legislators as well as common-law rules. These laws are constantly being changed to reflect the changing customs and desires of Americans.

We have federal laws that affect all the people in our country. We have state laws that affect only the people living or traveling in a given state or doing business with that state. We even have local laws that affect just the people in one city or county or district.

Different Ways Laws Are Created

Case Law, Also Called Common Law or Unwritten Law

Some early laws grew from decisions that judges made when someone came before them with a problem that did not seem to be covered in our law codes. Perhaps there was not a written law that clearly solved that particular problem. A judge might make a ruling based on what most persons would think was right. That is, the judge followed the customs and unwritten rules of the community.

If a similar case arose later with a similar question, lawyers might *cite* that first ruling (point it out). Then the judge hearing the second case could use it as a basis for decision. But the first ruling had to be cited and applied anew for each similar case. When a large number of judges had decided the same question in the same way, the decision became law. That first decision is called *setting a precedent*, and much of the study of law consists of reading about earlier decisions or precedents.

Case law, then, is a body of rules based on the written records of judges' decisions. Case law is made by judges rather than by legislators. We also call case law *common law.* To change such law, the courts might issue a decision *overriding the precedents*, bringing the law into line with changing social conditions.

Statutory Law, Which Is Written Law

The second type of law is called *statutory law.* It comes to us in the form of written laws or acts with exact words and rulings. These laws are drafted and approved by a federal, state, or local legislature, or by an administrative agency of the government.

REGULATIONS BY AGENCIES

As technology became more sophisticated and as science expanded beyond known truths, the common law did not provide sufficient controls for the rights and safety of the American people. Bureaus and agencies were set up to regulate these technologies as they grew. Laws are often made from *administrative rulings* of these agencies. Here are some examples:

- The Food and Drug Administration makes and enforces laws to assure purity, effectiveness, and truthful labeling of foods, drugs, and cosmetics sold in the United States.

- A local Board of Health rules on conditions which it oversees, such as the purity of water, standards of cleanliness, conditions of restaurants, and so on.

The Board can force a restaurant to shut down if it does not obey the ruling.

- The F.A.A. (Federal Aviation Administration) controls airlines, air traffic, and licensing. All aircraft and airports are governed by many F.A.A. rules of safety.

- The F.C.C. (Federal Communication Commission) regulates radio, television, cable, and wire communication. They set standards, create laws, guidelines, and licenses, and monitor violations.

- The Federal Maritime Commission regulates foreign and domestic shipping in American waters.

- The Interstate Commerce Commission is a federal agency which regulates matters of surface transportation (such as railroads, trucks, and buses).

The agencies mentioned above, and many other agencies, can have people arrested, fined large amounts of money, or have their businesses or housing shut down if they have abused regulations.

PROPOSING A NEW LAW IN THE CONGRESS

A *bill* is a proposed law (statute) which is being considered by the legislature but has not been enacted. Bills may be introduced only by members of Congress, but they can originate in different ways. They may be recommended by the president to party leaders or to Congress. They may be *framed* (drawn up) by congressional committees, or they may be the result of proposals by citizens, lobbyists, or special groups. Public opinion can strongly influence legislation. But only a senator or a representative can actually introduce a bill.

In general, a bill may be introduced in either the Senate or House of Representatives, but revenue bills (bills about taxes) must originate in the House. That is because a law about money, such as taxes that the people must pay, should fittingly come from the House, which is much larger than the Senate and most represents the people.

WHEN A BILL BECOMES A LAW

It is a long process from the time a bill is proposed to the time it is passed as a law. The bill must be studied and carefully considered in legislative committees. It must be discussed from many points of view by each house before the votes can be taken. If it passes both houses, the bill must be sent to the president for approval. The process can be hard to understand just with words. In the Activities and Games section of this book, I have described it in "Creating a Law." Instead of just reading how it is done, you might want to act out the whole process.

When a law is passed, unless there is an emergency, the law goes into effect at the end of the legislative session. That means that at a certain point the people must obey that law. There is a section in the Constitution about "ex post facto" laws. *Ex post facto* is a Latin term meaning "a thing done afterward." The Constitution provides that a person or company cannot be punished for doing something against the law if they did it *before* the law went into effect. If we make a new law about driving with seat belts, you cannot get arrested because you did not wear seat belts five years ago. If we make a new law about pollution, you cannot be arrested because your company polluted the streams near your factory two years ago.

As you have seen, it is not easy to get a law passed. Suppose that candidate who promised to close the schools really did get elected. We could be pretty sure that his bill would never get the necessary votes in the Congress—but only if the other members were wise! It is up to you and me to see that we send good men and women to represent us.

Laws May Adapt to Changing Times

As our society becomes larger and more crowded, more and more laws are created. Most laws we never think of, but they are there protecting us as we go about our daily lives. Some laws we think about very often.

Let's use traffic laws as an example of laws we are constantly aware of. We think about traffic laws because we know that if we break them we might get a ticket or citation, and we might have an accident. We also know that we are responsible for our actions while driving. If someone were to be killed because of our bad driving, it would be a terrible burden of guilt. And we could be charged with manslaughter or even murder. We also know that in order to drive, you will have to learn about those laws, get a driving license, and agree to drive lawfully.

> Driving is a privilege—not a right. It is subject to obeying all laws.

In order to obtain a driver's license you must pass a written test on traffic laws, signs, and safety. You must pass an eye test and a driving test. You must also prove your vehicle is safe and insured. Your signature on the license is an implied consent to the laws of liability (you agree to take responsibility for your actions).

If we drive and come upon a red light, we know that we must stop. Would it make sense if we demand our rights, our freedom to do whatever we please, and just race through that traffic light? No. As good drivers, we choose to give up some of our freedom and stop while the light is red. We also know that when the light changes to green, the cars going the other direction will stop at their red light. Then we can cross safely. It is common sense to obey traffic laws, not just to avoid a ticket, but so we can reach our destination in peace and in one piece. It is a choice we make.

Traffic laws are not just for drivers of motor vehicles. We must observe these laws when we are walking, skateboarding, or riding our bicycles. A walker who goes against a red light can cause a terrible accident—even deaths—and face prosecution and lawsuits. If you use your skateboard on the sidewalk and hit someone, you can face criminal charges and lawsuits.

Driving laws are easy to talk about. They are logical and based on safety. And they are an example of the kind of law that keeps changing over time. Now I am going to repeat myself to make a point. Remember what I told you about the way the common law works? How judges enforce the customs of a community? Sometimes a court comes upon a situation that is different from most, and there are no earlier case-decisions to be studied. The judge then must make a ruling which he or she considers just, and which agrees with the customs and opinions of the community. After this, if the same situation comes before a court, the first ruling which was recorded can be used as a basis for the next ruling. That first ruling is called a precedent. When a rule has been uniformly applied in a number of cases, it becomes part of the common law. Driving laws are an example.

When the first automobiles appeared on the streets, we didn't yet have any laws about using them, though we did have many rules or laws about the use of horses and wagons or carriages. Things became pretty confusing. Those old cars were noisy and often scared the horses. People felt they went too fast! And there were no road signs or traffic signals, no rules or laws at all about the automobile. So as disagreements came up, as accidents happened, as complaints were brought to court, people wanted some legal guidance.

Judges had to make the judgments or rulings, and they based them on common sense. There were unwritten rules about courtesy, safety, sharing, and taking turns. Applying these rules to what was going on helped judges make their decisions.

Later when similar cases came before the courts, lawyers often referred to previous decisions. They pointed out the earlier ruling as a precedent, as an example. As circumstances changed, laws changed. Those first drivers were lucky if they could get their cars to go ten miles an hour. And they thought that was fast—really fast. Speeding laws were made to limit those old cars. Now we have trouble holding our speed down to a fifty-five miles-per-hour speed limit. Times certainly changed, and so did those earlier speeding laws.

Ordinary Citizens as Lawmakers

Our joint power and responsibility to vote is why I care about you, why I care how you will vote when you are old enough. I don't even know your name, yet you are important to me. Your one vote is so very important, for you will be helping to decide what kind of a world I'll be sharing with you. What you do, how you think, affects me. We are sharing the same space at the same time. I want this world to be just and happy for myself and for others—people I don't even know!

Citizens can propose laws to their member of Congress—and hope he or she will propose them to the House or Senate. You can see how important it is to vote for a person whose ideas you respect. Another way to propose a law is to take it directly to the voters. To do this the people interested must write out the law as they want it passed and then get signatures of other citizens. This becomes an initiative or a proposition, as mentioned in Chapter 6. When enough signatures are collected, the proposed law will appear on the ballot in the next election for the voters to consider. This is one way the ordinary citizen has the right and the power to form our government.

A terrific example of voter power is the story of how citizen's rights were won for slaves. When the Constitution was being written, black people were not thought about. Most of them were slaves and not considered as having rights.

A lot of citizens wanted to do something about the unjust situation of slavery. The black people couldn't even vote. New laws were passed because the men who could vote wanted to do what was right. They didn't say, "Hey! Why should I care? I'm not black. That is their problem!"

When enough citizens declared that slavery was wrong, government leaders listened. In some states slavery was out-lawed, but in many states the voters wanted to keep the slaves. Arguments went on and on, until the slave states de-cided to leave the union. The government in Washington did not believe the United States should be broken up. The two sides went to war over the issue. Even after that terrible Civil War when so many young men had been killed and the slaves were finally declared free, black people were still not treated as equal in many states. Their rights were not acknowledged in many places.

It took a few more years for amendments to the Constitu-tion to be written assuring the equal rights of black people and their privileges as citizens, including the vote. None of this could have happened unless a lot of good voters got involved. They demanded that their representatives in Con-gress take these actions.

The Thirteenth Amendment to the Constitution declared that no one could be treated as a slave. Many people think this amendment declared the black person free. Actually, freedom could not be *granted* to the black person. No one had the right to take it away in the first place. Freedom was his right—his *birthright,* and not something that anyone has the power to take away. The Thirteenth Amendment is an example of people changing a law, or making a legal promise to change a bad situation.

In a similar way, laws to assure the rights of women and children were first brought about by fair-minded men, when men were the only ones who could vote.

I have a bumper sticker that says, "Voters Make History!" Indeed we do.

Chapter 8
KINDS OF LAW

We have a pretty clear understanding now of what is meant by *common law*, based on previous court decisions, and by *statute law*, made up of laws written and adopted by the legislature. But in courts of justice the law can also be thought of in other ways. Many kinds of law are practiced in the courts, but the most common are *civil law* and *criminal law*.

Civil Law

When you have a legal problem that does not involve breaking the law it is called a *civil matter*, and you want a civil trial. This kind of law regulates how people act with each other.

Lawyers handle civil matters in and out of court. Many legal disputes are settled in attorneys' offices and never reach a court. Sometimes an attorney who does not represent either side will come into the case as a *mediator*. That means that he or she will listen to both sides and offer compromises. Then perhaps both clients will feel that this is a better solution than going through an expensive and often emotionally difficult court trial.

If the matter does go to court, it is called a *civil suit* or *lawsuit*, and the outcome will be decided by a judge or jury.

The kinds of cases that are settled in civil law are:

- Torts: dealing with wrongful injury because of one's actions.

- Property: involving the rights and obligations of the individual who owns property.

- Contracts: dealing with business agreements between people.

- Inheritance: concerning the transfer of property upon death of the owner.

- Family Law: about the rights and obligations of a husband and wife and children.

- Corporation: law as it affects businesses and corporations.

- Public Law (Civil): involving the government directly with the laws of the land.

- Constitutional Law: concerning those rights spelled out in the constitutions of the federal and state governments.

- Administrative Law: involving the operation of governmental agencies.

- International Law: dealing with actions of other countries as they affect the United States of America and its citizens.

Some Instruments of Civil Law

A last will and testament is an example of a formal statement, an *instrument,* that may be brought into a civil court case. A corporation has articles of incorporation. There are many such instruments. Among the most common are titles and deeds, and patents and copyrights.

TITLE

A *title* is legal evidence of ownership. It is a term used to describe ownership, and it is the way an owner obtains lawful possession to property. It describes a deed to real property (land or building), title-ownership of an automobile, a patent for an invention, or a copyright for a writer, composer, or other creator of a work.

We often think of property as something we can see or touch. But there are other kinds of property. In law, the term *intellectual property* is used. The value of intellectual property is not in the actual product but in its concept, or the idea behind it. For instance, suppose you somehow got the formula to make Coca-Cola, and you went to Pepsi-Cola to sell this formula or recipe. The value to Pepsi is not the few cents-worth of paper and ink on which you wrote the recipe. The value is in the idea you wrote on that paper. If you are a spy and steal the plans for a super-secret new atomic missile, what you sell to the enemy is not the paper, ink, and paper clip. Although they get that also, it is the idea or plan that makes the paper so very, very valuable.

PATENTS

A *patent* gives an inventor exclusive right to an invention for a certain time. A patent allows an inventor to prevent others from making, selling, or using his or her invention in every country in which it is patented. It gives the inventor *title* to the invention.

To be eligible for a patent, an invention must be new and useful. Patent laws consider inventions to include machines, tools, methods, processes, products, and substances. It includes designs and new varieties of plant life.

Patent applications must include specific drawings, a list of claims that tell how the invention is used and what it will do. It includes a declaration that the inventor was the first person to create the invention. To get a patent requires specialized legal knowledge. You need the services of a patent attorney or patent agent.

COPYRIGHTS

A *copyright* is an author's legal right to protect what he or she has created. This was granted by Congress in 1790. It covers books, periodicals (magazines and journals), lectures, musical compositions, maps, works of art, drawings or models of a scientific nature, motion pictures, and sound recordings. It grants legal title to the creator of a work and enables the creator to sell, give, or even destroy this work. It prevents others from claiming ownership or authorship of a work.

DEEDS

A *deed* is a statement in writing that transfers the ownership of real estate (land) and things attached to it (like a building), either by sale or by gift. It must be signed by the person directly involved in the agreement, and it must be delivered. The deed must give an adequate description of the real estate and show intent to transfer the property. The buyer has the deed recorded by a registrar of deeds for the county. Before a deed can be recorded, it must be acknowledged by a public official called a notary public, who has the power to witness an oath. The seller acknowledges a deed by swearing to the notary public that he is selling the property of his own free will. This acknowledgment is not absolutely necessary to make a deed legal and is not always done, but it gives maximum protection to the buyer.

Criminal Law (Public Law)

Most practice of public law concerns breaking the law, the intervention of peace-keeping forces, and public prosecution. This is called *criminal law*, or we could say *public law*. It deals with actions that are harmful to society. It involves the body of rules or laws that we are commanded to obey and our methods of enforcing those laws.

When someone breaks a law, or if there is a strong reason to believe that has happened, then the person is *charged* with breaking the law. He or she has the right to a trial during which the government will try to prove the allegation (accusing statement). Criminal law is prosecuted by "the people" (the government).

Criminal law in the United States is an *accusatory process*, one in which we accuse someone of a deed and then we must prove it. That person is presumed innocent until we prove the claim or accusation. Many other nations have an *inquisitory* system, which means that if the government agents suspect someone of a crime, they bring him in and try to make him admit he is guilty. Sometimes this is done by torture. The burden of proof is on the accused—that means he must *prove* himself innocent or he will be punished as guilty. He must be able to obtain this proof of innocence even if he has no money or power or help. He must prove his innocence while being held in jail or prison. That is a really tough and unjust system.

The most exciting aspect of our American system of justice is that a person is presumed innocent unless he or she is *proved* guilty. This is surely one of our most valued rights.

Child Labor Law

We have a special field of law to protect children from bad working conditions. Children have been used as workers throughout history. On farms, in stores, and in family businesses, the children of the family were expected to help. This type of work was not wrong. But when we use the term *child labor* we usually mean the exploitation of young workers, often in factories or mines. *Exploitation* was the taking advantage of children in terrible conditions for unfair pay. The people who hired them knew that the children came from desperately poor families. These parents could not buy food or pay the rent without the money the children brought home. This made it easy for the employers to exploit the children. Child labor law came about because of the dreadful conditions in which some children worked. People became aware of this in the early 1700s and 1800s and called for change.

Within the factories there were terrible cases of abuse, but most of the public didn't know what was going on. Often, those who did know didn't want to do anything to stop it. Some business owners were greedy, and people who bought things liked the low prices. They didn't care how the products were made.

During the Industrial Revolution (when power machinery had just been invented), factories were set up to mass-produce all sorts of things. Many workers were needed to work the machines. The factory owners were anxious to make their products at the cheapest cost to themselves. Factories were often enormous buildings, unsafe, poorly ventilated, and poorly lighted. They were crowded with noisy machinery and hundreds of workers, many of whom were children.

Children were going to work so early in the morning that it was still dark—and they would work the whole long day until it was very late at night. Some children were forced to work with unsafe machines, and terrible accidents happened. Children who fell asleep were punished, often by having a pot of ice-cold water splashed in their faces. Some children were even chained to their machines.

Tiny boys worked in coal mines in tunnels under the earth. It was found that when they bent over they could fit into spaces too small for a grown man, so they were placed there and paid only pennies for hours of hard work. In the new cloth factories, children were hired to work large weaving machines. The owners of the businesses wanted to hire children because they could pay them less, and often children had the delicate hands necessary to handle the thousands of threads that fed into the weaving looms. It was dangerous work.

Working children didn't go to school. Most could neither read nor write. They never had a day off, so they didn't have any idea what was going on in the outside world. They would return home each night with only enough energy to eat a bit and fall on their beds to sleep. They never played.

Sometimes a poor family would get work from the factory and bring it home. They set up a shop in their houses and the whole family, even the tiniest children, would work day and night.

It is easy for us to understand that this was wrong. We live in a time where children have rights and laws to protect them. But in those days, many of these families were immigrants to this country. They were penniless and had no one to represent them. Many could not speak English. The streets of big cities were crowded with these new people who were desperate for places to live and jobs to pay for housing and food. Landlords often charged very high rents for small, terrible apartments. Families felt trapped. One of the worst things about child labor was that it not only robbed children of their childhood, but it took work away from adults. Children were an ideal group to exploit. They did not know anything except to do what they were told.

To many Americans, child labor was a dreadful sickness in the nation. Strong laws had to be passed. Some states passed laws, but it was hard to enforce them. Families were so poor that they didn't want to expose the abuse for fear the children would lose their jobs. Owners of businesses hid the truth behind the walls of their factories. Many politicians said it was good for these children to work. They said, "They came from other lands and probably wouldn't have much of a chance to do well anyway."

In 1802, the British Parliament passed the first law regulating child labor in England. The law forbade the employment of pauper children under nine years of age. Pauper children under fourteen could not work at night, and their workday was limited to twelve hours. Pauper children were those whose families could not support them or who had no parents. Pauper children were supposed to be placed for training with local tradesmen or craftsmen. But some communities were sending these children to factories where they worked under bad conditions and had no chance to learn a trade. The 1802 law covered only pauper children, and it was not even enforced. Still, it was a beginning, and it was followed by stronger laws. Then Americans who wanted social change became more active to make some strong laws here.

Massachusetts passed the first child labor law in the United States in 1836. The law prohibited the employment of children under fifteen years of age in any factory unless the children had attended school for at least three months during the year before. But by 1860, only a few states had outlawed factory employment of children under ten or twelve years of age.

Social workers, teachers, writers, labor leaders, and some business owners insisted that Congress pass effective legislation. A Child Labor Committee was established in 1904. Noted leaders became involved, such as Jane Addams, and they alerted the nation to these shocking conditions. It was obvious that strong legislation had to be enacted and enforced nationwide. It was felt that child labor laws must come from the federal government in Washington, D.C.

In 1916 the first federal child labor law was passed, which set standards for the hiring of children by industries involved in interstate or foreign commerce. In 1918 the Supreme Court declared that law unconstitutional, ruling that Congress had no power to regulate interstate commerce. More laws were made only to be overturned by the Supreme Court, which said that child labor laws denied the children their freedom to work if they wished.

The people working for justice continued the fight. Finally strong laws were passed and enforced. Children today are protected by many laws that set a minimum age for general employment, a higher minimum age for hazardous work, and limitations on the daily and weekly hours of work.

The story of child labor laws is a good example of people getting out and using their power. People insisted that their members of Congress listen to them. They worked hard to get the information to all the voters.

There are still some problems, though. For example, these days, many farm workers now travel from farm to farm picking crops. They often have their children out in the fields picking with them. The children do not regularly attend school. Their families rarely stay in one place long enough for the child to attend one school. These families are very poor, and the children's wages help them to live.

This is a problem you might want to investigate and report to your newspapers. You could write to your legislators. Your school class could take this on as a project and involve other schools throughout your state and the nation. Perhaps you do not live in a farm area, but are aware of other kinds of child-labor abuses. Do something. You are important and you have power!

Some Strange Laws

Many laws that seem strange to us now were quite sensible in the olden days. But laws can become out of date, and then they can seem very funny. Some have never been taken off the books, though they are never used. Here are some examples:

- In Burns, Oregon, horses are allowed in the town's saloons, but only after the rider pays an admission fee for the animal.

- One town required that after the sun went down all horses must carry at least one taillight. (That sounds okay to me, except where do they attach them?)

- In Idaho, anyone over the age of eighty-eight is not permitted to drive a motorcycle.

- All bicycles in Pueblo, Colorado, must carry gongs!

- In Oklahoma it is against the law to read a comic book while driving. (Hmmm, is it legal to read other books while driving?)

- If a married woman lives in Michigan, she isn't allowed to cut her own hair without her husband's permission.

- In Ohio, passengers are forbidden by law from riding on the roof of a taxi.

- In Florida a woman is forbidden by law to fall asleep while sitting under a hair dryer.

- In Green Bay, Wisconsin, it is illegal to have a car that drips oil on the road, and the fine is one dollar for each drop!

- A law in Arkansas states that an automobile on the road must have a man walking ahead of it and waving a red flag.

- A person caught double-parking in Minnesota can be put on a chain gang and fed only bread and water.

- In Oklahoma it is against the law to fire a gun that is not loaded.

- A couple of states have laws forbidding persons from lying down and napping in the middle of the road.

- In one town it is illegal to shave in the middle of the road.

Back to Serious Ideas about Law

It's fun to read about old laws that were made in the days when life was very different in this country. But it's more important to know what the law means today. We've covered what a law is, who makes our laws, how these laws are made, and what the different kinds of laws are. In the next chapter we'll talk about what you can do if you do not like a law, if you think a law is unjust or unfair.

Chapter 9
TO CHANGE A LAW

What can you do if you don't like a statute or law? Suppose you think a law is wrong? Do you have any choices in this government of, by, and for the people? Sure, you have many. Let's explore.

Changing a Law through Legislation

We have said that one of the ways to change a law is by legislation. When the people want a law changed they can ask their lawmakers for a *repeal*, which will cancel the law, or they can ask for the law to be *amended* (changed).

Now, let's talk about our lawmakers. Remember who makes the laws? We are thinking here about statutory laws, not common law. Remember the difference? (It's explained on pages 22 and 23 in Chapter 7.) Members of our Senate and House of Representatives work for us in Washington D.C. and make our federal laws. The people of each state have their own legislators who make the state laws. Counties, cities, and small towns elect people who make laws that affect just the people of their area.

And remember how these lawmakers got their jobs. Yes, you elected them, or at least you will when you are old enough to vote. Then it will be important to know what these people stand for and how they think, and what they say they will do for you. And I want to say over and over, "Become informed and be sure to vote!".

Back to this law you don't like. You can write or visit your lawmaker (senator or representative) and tell him or her what you think. The member of Congress-will probably listen or read your letter. You might even receive an answer. But you have just one vote. Unless your argument is very convincing, I'm not sure the legislator will work hard to change that law just for you.

A group, such as a certain business or profession that wants to benefit by certain laws, may hire a lobbyist. *Lobbyists* are people who are paid to go to our lawmakers and try to persuade them to vote a certain way. Lobbyists must register to let people know which group they represent and what their interests are.

But suppose you, yourself, want to make a larger impression on the lawmaker. Suppose you write a petition, a formal paper that tells what you think about that law. Then you get five thousand other voters to agree with you and sign your paper, and you send it to your lawmaker. Those five thousand signatures mean five thousand votes! I am quite sure you will get a good deal of attention.

Every vote is precious. Even if you are the only one who feels as you do—go ahead and use that power of the vote. As a person who believes in the ideals of justice, you need to use every opportunity to exercise your power. It is possible that some people would use their vote, their power, to make bad laws. Thank heavens there are also many good-thinking citizens who, like you, can make sure that bad laws don't happen.

Changing a Law by Direct Action

Laws can also be changed by direct action of the people. One way is to submit the proposed law or proposed change to the voters. As mentioned before, this is called an initiative or a ballot proposition. The people wanting change must get a certain number of signatures on a petition which states what they want. This requires a very large number of signatures, but if that many people want the change it will be put on the ballot and offered to all the citizens for a vote.

Another way to change a law is for a citizen to bring a test case against any law he or she believes is unconstitutional. In other words, the person can deliberately act against the law and then defend himself in court by arguing that the law is wrong according to the Constitution. He or she may take the case as high as the Supreme Court. If the court agrees that the law is wrong, it will be rescinded (it will no longer be a law), and the person who brought the test case will not be punished.

The Important Rights of Assembly and Petition

You can also do many things right in your own community. You can protest, make your feelings known, carry signs, march, make speeches, demonstrate. But do it legally! Do not break a law to protest a law (by hurting someone or destroying property, for instance). The First Amendment to our Constitution says:

> Congress shall make no law prohibiting or abridging the right of people peaceably to assemble and to petition the government for a redress of grievances.

This *redress of grievances* means simply to tell the government what you think is wrong or what you think they are doing wrong. It means that you can ask for a correction of something that you think is unfair. In some countries you would be put in jail for doing so.

There are limits to the process of *assembly and petition*. The word *peaceably* is part of the right guaranteed in the First Amendment. This means that our meetings and demonstrations should be peaceful. They shouldn't pose a threat to others or their property. Local, state, and national governments have enacted certain laws to keep peace and order. The U.S. Supreme Court has held that these laws must be reasonable. As an example, in many cities people who are planning to march or demonstrate must get permits to do so.

Think of Martin Luther King, Jr. He set out to overcome grievances of the black people in this country. He led peaceful demonstrations and marches, for which he asked and was given permission. His followers obeyed the rules about where they were allowed to march, where they could give speeches and demonstrate.

He also encouraged his followers to boycott (refuse to buy) and strike (refuse to work). Many black workers did not show up for work, and the businesses had to shut down. It was a legal way to show the rest of the community that they couldn't get along without the cooperation of the black people. When the black people boycotted certain businesses, the business owners found how important black shoppers were. They saw that they needed them to spend their money, or their businesses would fail.

When black people demonstrated, many lawmakers thought at first that just a few unhappy people were marching around and making some speeches. The television networks didn't pay much attention either, until they suddenly realized that this wasn't some little group of black people. As the Civil Rights Movement grew, the demonstrations grew. The newspapers and television networks realized there were thousands and thousands of people participating. And it wasn't just black people who were there. There were people of all races and ages, and men and women and children.

Just because this was a "black issue" didn't mean that people of all races were not involved. Most people want to live in a society that is based on equality, with the rights of everyone guaranteed. When television showed those thousands of people (and remember that means thousands of votes), the lawmakers paid attention. Many unjust laws and conditions were changed.

So What If *You* Don't Like a Law?

If we have a law you don't like, change it. You can demonstrate, protest, strike, appeal to your lawmaker, petition, write to newspapers. But do it legally!

I have mentioned quite a few ways you can change a law. Now there is still something you can do if you don't like a law. Something we have not mentioned yet—give up? Read on.

> Okay. You can *break* that law. I said that if you do not like a law, you can choose to break it. Yes you can!

But if you do, you can get arrested!

The next chapter of this book begins to explain *exactly* what happens when a person chooses to break the law.

Chapter 10
WHEN PEOPLE BREAK THE LAW

In this chapter and the three that follow it, we will look at the main facts about arrest and court trial of persons who are accused of breaking the law. After that, a chapter explains the special features of juvenile law, the procedures for young people who get into trouble.

Here's a true story about what happened when some boys went out to break the law. They carried knives. Maybe they didn't plan to kill anyone, but surely they meant to break the law against hurting other people.

> The two boys crept through the park looking for the guys who insulted their friend. They had knives and wore combat boots and fatigue clothing. They came upon a poor old homeless man who was sleeping on the grass. Suddenly he sat up and startled the boys, who then stabbed him eleven times. The old man died.
>
> The boys were on some emotional "high." They imagined themselves tough and powerful, and above right and wrong, when they entered the park. They darkened their knives so the blades wouldn't shine in the moonlight. They felt really tough. After the stabbing they wiped the blood off the blades on the grass. Then they went back to their boarding school and bragged and described every detail. They said, "Smell my boots, smell the blood!" They were caught up in the drama and had lost

touch with reality. They were not high on drugs or any other substance, just their own madness.

Other students called the police, who arrived quickly. The police advised the boys of their rights, especially the right to remain silent, but the boys ranted on and on. They told the whole story. Later, when they calmed down after being taken to jail, they realized the seriousness of their situation. When they appeared before the judge and were asked how they answered the charges, they said, "Not guilty, Your Honor."

When I attended the trial, I saw the boys weeping as the police tape recorder played their confession. While their voices described the stabbing over and over, the district attorney kept plunging the knife into the chest of a clothing-store dummy—eleven times. The jury was stunned.

Your Choice, Your Responsibility

If you choose to break a law, then you must take the consequences. When you choose to break a law you know that you can be arrested and there will be certain punishments if you are proved guilty. The boys in the above true story were sentenced to seventeen years in prison.

Be aware that if you break a law it is by choice. Your choice. If you break the law, you choose to do it willingly. Of course, everything is not clear and simple. Let's talk about that word *willingly* that I just used. It means that you do something of your own free will, and that involves using your brain. It means thinking that choice out. How many times have we heard people say, "Think before you act."?

What happens if you give your choice away? Suppose you tell someone that you will do everything they tell you to do. If you do something against the law, who gets the blame? Who gets arrested? Yes, you do! What if your boss or leader or even your president tells you to do something you think is wrong? You must think it out very carefully.

Giving away your ability to choose is one of the biggest problems of belonging to a gang. Many gang members do things they would never do if they were alone. They go along with things when everyone seems to be doing it, or if they are told they must do these acts. Sometimes a new gang member is told to break the law to prove he or she is part of "them."

The answer is to think for yourself. You are responsible for your actions. And if you are arrested and sent to jail—you go there all alone. Your friends or other gang members don't go to jail with you (unless two or more joined in the crime like the boys in the story). No, if you were on your own, your friends just wave good-bye. Sure, they may think you are real tough, that you did real good. But while you are sitting in jail, they are out in the sunshine saying how cool you were. Well, jail is not cool.

Jail can be really terrible. It is not just because the guards may be unfriendly, or because the food is not what you like. It is terrible to lose your freedom. It is terrible to live that close to other people twenty-four hours a day. It is terrible to never have privacy, to never have perfect quiet, to never be alone, to be told when to eat and when to sleep and what to do every day. You share your time and space with other prisoners who chose poorly and who may be very angry. You are someone on whom they can take out their anger. And remember: people often do things when they are in a group that they would never do if they were all alone.

Remember Chapter 4 in this book, on *Control*? When we talk about choosing to break the law, we are really talking about the idea of control. Who you put in control is your choice. If you don't like people bossing you around all the time, then take control of yourself. It's that easy.

Most of us do not need policemen or anyone watching us all the time. We do not need to be told when we may move and when to stop, what to do and how to do it. And yet there are people who need such control. These are persons who are not in control of themselves. They live peaceably and obey the laws only when they are told, when they are controlled by others. That is why we have jails and prisons.

Actions for Which a Person Can Be Cited or Arrested

There are two main classes of criminal offenses.

- Misdemeanor: a criminal offense less serious than a felony, generally punishable by a fine or limited time in a county jail—or both.

- Felony: a crime more serious than a misdemeanor, usually punishable by imprisonment in a state penitentiary for more than a year and/or by substantial fines.

Most unlawful acts are explained in the list below:

- Arson: the burning of property, such as a building, causing harm without legal justification or excuse.

- Assault: an unlawful attempt on the person of another, coupled with an ability to commit a violent injury. You do not have to actually connect or commit the act. The threat is the crime.

- Assault with a Deadly Weapon: assault with a weapon, which makes the crime much more serious. It is a felony.

- Battery: an assault that causes injury. Battery is the act of injuring the victim. Both assault and battery can be felonies. The victim can also sue the person who did the action in a civil suit and perhaps collect *damages* (an award of money established by the court).

- Burglary: the entering of any structure with the intent to commit theft or any other felony. The definition differs a bit from state to state, but essentially it is the unlawful entering of someone's property.

- Child Abuse: the act of willfully causing or permitting a child to suffer needlessly, or inflicting unjustifiable physical or mental suffering, or having the care or custody of any child and willfully causing or permitting the child to be placed in peril.

- Cruelty to Animals: any action that causes excessive pain needlessly to an animal.

- Disturbing the Peace: unusual fighting or doing something to disturb such as loud or unreasonable noise; or words that are likely to provoke someone into violence, such as calling someone a name that will greatly disturb that person or others.

- Driving Under the Influence (D.U.I.): driving when a person's blood-alcohol level is measured at .08 or above (this level might be different in some states). That .08 means eight-tenths of one percent—that is very little alcohol. When someone is killed by a driver who is proved to be driving under the influence, the district attorney will usually bring charges. It is hard to prove "Murder 1" (Murder in the First Degree—see definition below). Murder requires malice, and Murder 1 requires planning ahead. When a person is drunk, his or her thinking process is muddled. The accident probably is not intentional. But nevertheless, the driver is responsible. If the victim dies in a drunk driving accident, the driver can be charged with "Murder 2" (Murder

in the Second Degree) or with Vehicular Manslaughter. Prison sentences can be up to seven,
eight, or nine years. The higher the driver's blood-
alcohol level was, the longer the prison sentence is
apt to be.

- Drugs—Under the Influence of an Illegal Substance: it is against the law to use illegal drugs. An
  arrest can be made if someone is observed by the
  police (after using an illegal drug or substance) and
  is determined to be under the influence. You do
  not have to be driving to be arrested for this
  offense.

- Embezzlement: the taking of something entrusted
  to you. This is most often in business matters,
  when your responsibility and honesty are assumed
  to be part of your position. It is not necessary to
  prove intent.

- Family Violence: it is a crime for any member or
  former member of a family or household to
  physically or mentally abuse someone within that
  family.

- Fraud: intentional deception to deprive another
  person of property or to injure that person in
  some other way.

- Homicide: the killing of one human being by
  another. It is regarded by our society as the most
  serious crime. See also "Manslaughter" and
  "Murder" below.

- Kidnapping: the forceful taking of a person and
  the holding of that person against his will. It is the
  unlawful carrying off of a person from his

residence, state, or country, usually for the purpose of ransom. It is a felony. Kidnapping is also a federal offense and is prosecuted by the federal government.

- Larceny: the unlawful taking and carrying away of someone else's personal property. If you take under $400 in value, the charge is a misdemeanor. If you take more than that, it becomes a felony.

- Manslaughter: a homicide without malice. This crime has two categories. Voluntary Manslaughter involves death with some level of responsibility on the part of the defendant. The charge might show an intent to kill in the heat of passion or a sudden quarrel. Involuntary Manslaughter involves no intent to kill; often it is an accidental death.

- Murder: the taking of another's life with malice, which means the intent to cause harm. It is malice that makes it murder. There are different degrees of murder. Also, if murder is committed in the course of a felony such as robbery, rape, burglary, or other unlawful act, it is called *Felony Murder*, and the consequences can be much more serious.

- Murder in the First Degree (Murder 1): a defendant is charged with Murder 1 if the district attorney thinks there is premeditation, deliberation, and intent to kill. That means that the murder was planned and not just an accident. The punishment can be prison for twenty-five years to life, or it can be death.

- Murder in the Second Degree (Murder 2): the charge is Murder 2 if the district attorney thinks there was killing with malice, but the intent to kill did not exist until just before the crime. This involves no premeditation and no deliberation.

- Rape: sexual intercourse with a woman or man without consent, and usually by force or deception. Statutory Rape is sexual intercourse with a person below the *age* of consent, even with consent.

- Robbery: the taking of personal property in the possession of another from his person or immediate presence, against his will, and accomplished by means of fear or force. Robbery is a felony, punishable by time in jail or prison depending on the circumstances of the crime. A fine can be imposed. Armed Robbery is the charge when a deadly weapon is used. This makes it even more serious in the eyes of the law.

- Shoplifting: the taking of any merchandise without paying for it. Shoplifting can be a felony or misdemeanor depending on the value of the object taken.

- Theft: a crime in which another person's property is taken with the intent to deprive the rightful owner. It can be Grand Theft, which is a felony, if something of great value or a large amount of money was taken. Petty Theft involves property of less value, and is usually a misdemeanor. However, with a prior arrest record, Petty Theft becomes a felony.

The Laws about Alcohol and Other Drugs

Crimes today are often related to use of alcohol or other drugs, so it is important to have more information about how such use can lead to arrest.

Being Under the Influence

It is against the law to drink alcohol before you reach the age of twenty-one, and it is illegal to sell or give liquor to a person below the age of twenty-one.

It is also against the law for anyone to be under the influence of illegal drugs. Therefore an officer can stop a suspect and administer a test if he or she thinks that person is under the influence.

The usual tests for alcohol are explained below, under "Driving Under the Influence (D.U.I.)." For other drugs, the officer can look for needle marks on the person or check the pupils of that person's eyes to see if they are dilated. If the pupils are unusually large or small the officer can infer drug use.

Driving Under the Influence (D.U.I.)

In most states there are two statutes for Driving Under the Influence.

1. It is against the law to drive at a time when you are under the influence of alcohol or drugs.

2. It is against the law to drive when your blood-alcohol level is .08 or higher—that means eight-tenths of one percent or higher. (California recently passed a law that a minor is considered D.U.I. with a blood alcohol level of .01.)

The exact laws about drinking and driving may differ a bit from state to state, but most of the laws are very similar. In California the arresting officer will warn you:

> "You are required by State Law to submit to a chemical test to determine the alcohol content of your blood. You have a choice of whether this test is to be of your blood, breath, or urine. If you refuse to submit to a test, or fail to complete a test, your driving privilege will be suspended for a period of six months. You do not have the right to talk to an attorney or have an attorney present before stating whether you will submit to a test, before deciding which test to take, or during the administration of the test chosen."

The reason you are not allowed an attorney at that time is because the effect of the alcohol could be gone if it took many hours for an attorney to appear.

When your blood-alcohol level is determined, the higher the level is, the more days you will spend in jail. A level of .08 or above is considered legally drunk, even if the person is not acting drunk. People react to alcohol differently and some are drunk even with a lower level. This is often the case with small people who weigh very little. A very large person might be able to drink more before reaching a blood-alcohol level of .08—but that is not true of everyone, and it is very important not to take a chance.

If someone is arrested for the first time for a D.U.I. violation, he or she will either be held in jail or be released with a citation (a ticket) which demands an appearance in court for arraignment. If convicted, he or she may be:

- Fined a large amount of money

- Told to attend driving school

- Told to attend Alcoholics Anonymous meetings

- Have his or her driver's license suspended

- Possibly sent to jail.

Some circumstances can make drunk driving even more serious. If someone is hurt because of the driver's drunkenness, the charge will be a felony. If someone is killed, the charge will be manslaughter or murder. If a person knows that he or she has a drinking problem, and does drink and drive, *intent* is shown, which will affect the guilt. For a fourth D.U.I. offense within seven years, the defendant could get three years in a state prison in most states.

The Crime Lab—Forensics

The chemical tests for blood-alcohol level and many other tests of evidence are done in a crime laboratory, where scientists work in an exciting field called *forensics*. Much of the work in a crime lab involves *forensic medicine*, the science concerned with the relation between medical knowledge and the law. Here's an example of how forensics can help the administration of justice:

> In 1984, Alec Jeffreys, a scientist in England, discovered *DNA typing*, a procedure for mapping the unique genetic code of an individual. No one is exactly like us except if we are one of identical twins.
>
> Jeffreys' laboratory in England was near the scene of a murder of two young girls. For four years investigators followed all clues and they came up with nothing. When the murder was discovered, some samples had been taken of blood that was on the girls but was not their own blood. Jeffreys applied his procedure to the problem of identifying this blood genetically. He compared the genes in the blood samples with genes in blood taken from the suspect.
>
> The blood matching freed a seventeen-year-old man who had been arrested as a prime suspect—and it led to the real killer, a psychopath named Colin Pitchfork. (This

case was written about in *The Blooding*, a best-selling book by Joseph Wambaugh.)

In 1990, 29,993 people were convicted of violent crimes in the United States. This number was up from 23,172 in 1986. Law enforcement is overwhelmed by the rapid increase in crime and is looking for newer and better ways for crime solving.

People often say that dead men tell no tales, but their bodies certainly reveal much for scientists to see. A scientist who works in a forensic laboratory may specialize in one of many areas. An *odontologist* could use bite marks to help confirm the identity of a killer. A *ballistics expert* pinpoints the specific gun used in a shooting. The *pathologist* studies many things including burn marks and the entry of a bullet to decide whether a death was murder or suicide. Forensics has come a long way since the early days when it just determined whether a death was natural or unnatural.

In the late nineteenth and early twentieth centuries, an explosion of discoveries brought science into the field of law enforcement. In France, Alphonse Bertillion started using *mug shots* (identification photos). Another Frenchman, Alexandre Lacassagne, discovered that each gun is unique. Drilling the hole in the barrel of the gun left the metal uneven, which scarred the bullet. No two guns made the same scar pattern on bullets, so it was easy to prove which gun fired a particular bullet. Scientists in Germany began the practice of bloodstain identification with a test that told the difference between animal blood and human blood. These days, we have specialists who can tell important things about bones, nails, and skin. Wonderful machines have been developed which aid in determining what substance a spot on cloth may be. Machines can analyze stains, powder burns, foods, and blood.

By mid-1988, United States law enforcement officials had become very excited about a new investigative technique called *DNA testing*. It was based on the procedures developed by Alec Jeffreys, as told in the story beginning this section.

DNA testing has been called the most powerful investigative tool of the twentieth century. The term *DNA fingerprinting* is sometimes used because each person has a different genetic pattern or code, just as each person has a different pattern of fingerprints. Genetic profiling (forming an idea or impression of a person from genetic clues) quickly moved into United States courtrooms. In the last decade, DNA evidence has become a crucial part of the criminal-justice system and has been used in thousands of cases.

All this is pretty heavy science for you, and most adults haven't yet learned enough to understand it. It is new and it is exciting, and it is part of your future world. Let's see if I can explain just enough to let you understand.

The letters DNA stand for a big word, *deoxyribonucleic acid*. Every cell of our body contains DNA (except the red cells in the blood—but the white blood cells do have DNA). DNA is the chemical that forms the building blocks of genes, and genes are the blueprints for our bodies. Genes make our eyes blue or brown, our hair straight or curly, our bodies short or tall.

DNA can be taken from tiny traces of blood, saliva, semen, or hair found at a crime scene. The DNA can be analyzed by complicated laboratory tests to reveal a pattern that might look something like those bar-codes on the grocery items at the check-out counter. This pattern, from a substance found at the crime scene, can be compared with the DNA pattern of a suspect. If it is the same, it identifies the suspect as a person who was at the scene of the crime. This identification is considered to have a "high degree of certainty." DNA analysis has enabled law enforcement to solve cases that probably wouldn't be solved without it.

Because the use of DNA test results is new to the courtroom, law officers and judges are not always ready to accept this as the only evidence to convict someone. And it is possible (though not likely) for the test to yield false results. But as the technology improves and becomes better known, more and more courts will accept it. For you students, genetics will be a natural part of your education and your world.

Chapter 11
UNDER ARREST!

Your Responsibility

When you have broken the law and are arrested, it doesn't do any good to tell the arresting officer, "I couldn't help it!" or, "He made me do it!" You break the law by choice. There was other behavior you could have chosen. *You are responsible for your actions.*

If you give away your judgment or decision-making brain by drinking too much alcohol or taking drugs, are you still accountable for what you do? Does your responsibility *start* when you choose to abuse your brain with a substance? These are heavy thoughts for someone with the power to choose and the power to vote. Alcohol and drugs are involved in most crimes committed, and therefore are very important for us to think about.

It doesn't help to say that you didn't know that doing this or that was illegal. It is your responsibility to know what is against the law. For example, when you get your driver's license you must study and pass a test to prove that you know the traffic laws, so ignorance is not an excuse. You should also keep informed of other laws that affect you.

Okay, you have been caught breaking the law, or maybe you are just in a situation where it *looks* like you have broken the law. Either way, you have been arrested. That is a very frightening thing that none of us want to have happen. But at least we live in the United States, where we have certain "constitutional guarantees" to protect us.

Let's go over a few definitions again, before we get on with what happens when you are arrested. We are not talking about private, or civil, law in this chapter. (As I explained earlier, civil law is used when one person or business sues another.) Right now we are thinking about public law, which is the body of rules or laws in which our justice system is directly involved.

The most familiar part of public law is criminal law, the body of rules we are commanded to obey. The government may fine people who do not obey or send them to jail. In some states the government can even execute a convicted criminal. Criminal law is the set of rules that the government enforces through the justice system—our police, sheriffs, marshals, courts, and related agencies.

But as I said before, even if we break a law, we can feel assured that we have certain constitutional guarantees to protect us. In order to point these out, I will tell you about arrest, booking, and trial, and relate how constitutional guarantees affect what happens to someone who is arrested.

As we talk about arresting someone, it is important to remember:

> The Constitution guarantees that a person is considered innocent until proved guilty.

When Can a Person Be Arrested?

A person can be arrested when suspected of a crime if there is *probable cause*. Probable cause is determined when there are sufficient legal reasons for allowing the arrest of a person based upon *articulable facts* (that means based on facts that can be told clearly to justify the arrest). There are three basic situations in which someone can be arrested:

1. Perhaps the officer saw the person break the law and simply arrests him or her.

2. Perhaps the officer did not see the crime committed; but someone else saw it happen and can identify the person they saw doing it. The officer can listen to the story of the witnesses and make the judgment whether that suspect can be arrested. The officer needs enough proof (*probable cause*, also called *p.c.*) to petition a judge for a warrant.

3. Perhaps no one saw the crime committed, but there is proof that a crime happened. At this point the agency responsible, such as the police, would conduct an investigation. Evidence would be collected. If there was enough evidence and if it pointed to a specific person, this would establish probable cause. A warrant would be issued and the suspect could be arrested. It is important to remember the Fourth Amendment to the Constitution, which protects us from unreasonable search and seizure. That is why the police must have a warrant before they can enter someone's space and make an arrest or take property as evidence.

Arrest and Booking

At the time of arrest, the officer may subdue the suspect or apply handcuffs, even though the person being arrested is presumed innocent. This is because along with the suspect's rights, the rest of us also have rights. And if the officer feels that our safety is threatened, or that the suspect might run away, then he or she may (and usually does) handcuff the suspect.

The Miranda Warning

After subduing the suspect (putting him or her under control), the officer goes right back to insuring that person's rights as guaranteed by the Constitution. Probably you have all watched on television as the officer read the Miranda Warning to the suspect. This is a warning that if the suspect says anything, it may be used in court. Remember the case I described involving the two boys who were convicted of stabbing the homeless man in the park?

When a person is arrested, the officer must formally read the Miranda Warning. (There are exceptions as in emergencies or in the "heat of battle.")

"1. You have the right to remain silent.

2. Anything you say can be held against you in a court of law.

3. You have the right to talk to a lawyer and to have the lawyer present before and during questioning.

4. If you cannot afford to hire a lawyer, one will be appointed to represent you before and during questioning if you wish one."

After the warning, the following questions are asked and the reply is written next to each question. This is called securing a waiver.

"1. Do you understand each of these rights I have explained to you?

2. Having these rights in mind, do you wish to talk or not talk to us now?"

The Miranda Warning is important when the police want to question a suspect who is in custody (under arrest). If the officer questions the suspect about the crime and has not given the Miranda Warning, the conversation cannot be used as testimony in court. Even if the suspect starts talking about the crime without being questioned, the defense can ask for the suspect's statements to be excluded from the trial. So most officers give the warning as soon as they make an arrest.

Booked into Jail

After being given the Miranda Warning, the suspect (also called *the custody*) is taken to the police department for photographing and fingerprinting. He or she might be held in a temporary cell until being booked into jail. Booking procedures differ from county to county and from state to state, but usually go about as follows.

At the time of booking, the charges against the custody are filed and he is allowed to make phone calls. If the custody is to be kept, that is, not released on bail, then he is booked into jail. In some jails the defendant is allowed two phone calls if one is to a bail bond agency, otherwise only one call is allowed.

The defendant is given an identification (ID) number to help the people who work in the jail from mixing him with any other prisoner. His fingerprints are put through a computer, which should show if he is wanted in any other place on other charges. Some agencies give him a wristband with his picture and ID number.

All the items on the defendant are taken and put in a safe place until his release. The prisoner's clothing is removed and jail clothing is issued so he can be identified as easily as possible by jail personnel. The color and type of clothing might differ a bit within jails and prisons, but most often a nonconvicted prisoner is given a gray-colored shirt. Convicted prisoners wear dark blue shirts. Trustees wear green T-shirts. Prisoners on work programs are issued blue denim shirts.

Dangerous prisoners or prisoners who need special watching are given very brightly colored shirts or jump suits, usually a "day-glo" orange color. Recently some prisoners have been given red shirts, meaning "administrative isolation." This means it is thought unwise to put the person with others and may be used with gang members. Prisoners who have special health problems such as AIDS and TB are often dressed in white jump suits and are isolated. That means they do not share a cell with other prisoners.

In many prisons or jails, men prisoners are given light sandals. Women prisoners are given light tennis-type shoes. It is important that footwear is light so that if someone kicks another, the threat of injury is reduced. Prisoners are issued jeans, and all clothes including underwear and socks are marked with the word *jail* and often the name of the city or county.

Finally when the prisoner is ready, he is assigned to a cell, alone or shared with others. Convicted and nonconvicted prisoners are housed in different areas of the jail. Prisoners who are a danger to themselves or to others are isolated. Some prisoners are isolated because other prisoners might hurt them. Perhaps a suspect gave evidence in exchange for a lesser sentence. If he "snitched" or told on others, it is pretty certain they would want to get even with him. If he had to share a cell with them, he might be in danger. Even the other prisoners who were not directly involved might try to punish him.

Allegation and Arraignment— Going before the Judge

The Sixth Amendment of the Constitution guarantees us a *speedy and public trial*. That means if you are arrested, you won't be thrown into a cell and kept there for years until somebody gets around to your case. In some countries that is exactly what happens.

After an arrest the police start the paperwork that will tell about the suspect and the reason for arrest. It will list any criminal history the police might have about the person. It will list evidence or witness reports and any other information that will help the district attorney's office to make decisions about the case.

Under our law, a person must be brought before a judge within forty-eight hours of working-day time. (In some states the time is different. A few are trying to lower that to twelve hours.) When the accused is brought before a judge, he or she must be informed of the charges (accusation). The word *alleged* is used. "This is a case of alleged assault and battery," for example. The charge is called the *allegation*. This word means that the charge has not been proved. The process of coming before a judge within forty-eight hours is called an *arraignment*.

At the arraignment the judge advises the defendant of the charges against him (tells him what he is accused of), and asks the defendant if he wants a lawyer. The judge then asks the defendant whether he wants to plead guilty or not guilty. The defendant has been given time to talk to his attorney. Together they decide how he should answer.

Pleading Guilty

Often, in simple cases, the defendant pleads guilty at the arraignment and the sentence can be given at this time. If the defendant just wants to serve his "time" and get on with his life, he can plead guilty. No trial is needed, and the judge imposes the sentence. The judge is usually a bit easier than a jury would be if the defendant pleads guilty and seems to be sorry for what he did.

In more complicated cases, a date is set for sentencing if the defendant pleads guilty. Again, there is no need for a trial. It will take about a week for all the papers (the reports) on this person to be collected for the judge to study before sentencing. In complex or more serious cases, the time might be longer.

The judge wants to find out if this person has any prior (earlier) history of crime. He or she wants to see if this person has been living a responsible life and probably will not get into trouble again. The judge must decide on a just sentence, one that will satisfy society (at least get the person off the streets if he is dangerous or refuses to behave), and that conforms to the laws for such crimes. The Eighth Amendment protects a prisoner from cruel or excessive punishment. Cruel punishment would include forms of torture, and excessive punishment would be unreasonably long sentences for minor misdeeds. We certainly should not like a person to be beaten, put in jail for ten years, or even shot for stealing a loaf of bread. That is exactly what happens in some countries in this world, and has and still can happen in the United States if we are not always mindful of the rights of all our citizens.

Pleading Nolo Contendere (No Contest)

Sometimes a defendant will plead *nolo contendere* (no contest). This is not an admission of guilt, but it means that there will not be a trial. The defendant agrees to accept the sentence of the court. If he is sued in a civil suit following the criminal case, the plea cannot be used against him. Suppose a man was accused of drunk driving and he hurt someone. If he pleaded guilty, or if he was found guilty at a trial, the person who was hurt could sue him later in a civil suit for *damages* (an amount of money). By the no-contest plea, there won't be a criminal trial. If the injured person wants to sue the defendant, the charge will have to be proved in a civil trial.

Pleading Not Guilty

If the defendant pleads not guilty, the government will prosecute the case. During a trial, the prosecution is represented by the district attorney, and he or she or the deputies will try the case for you and me. You and I are referred to as *the people*. We, the taxpayers, pay for the district attorney's office and we also pay for the public defender's office, which provides a lawyer for a defendant who cannot afford to hire one.

To prosecute an alleged crime is to present evidence and testimony in an attempt to prove that the person is guilty. If the government didn't believe the defendant was guilty, it would hesitate to bring that person to trial.

For serious crimes, there may be a separate "sentencing trial" with a jury to decide on the punishment. For example, in a murder trial there is a possibility of life in prison or execution.

It is important for you to know that in criminal cases the "victim" is the people of the state or county, not the person who was actually robbed, beaten, or whatever. The person who suffered these bad things is a witness to tell the judge and jury that a crime occurred, and what happened. This idea should help encourage people to come forward when a crime happens. They don't need to feel bad about reporting crimes. They are not "snitching"—they are helping the government (they are the government).

The Right to Have a Lawyer

The defendant at the arraignment has already been advised that he is entitled to *counsel*, which means that he can have an attorney represent him. Remember that the officer told him this when he gave the Miranda Warning. The Sixth Amendment to the Constitution guarantees "the assistance of counsel." If the defendant cannot afford counsel (an attorney), one will be appointed from the public defender's office. If a town does not have a public defender, an attorney from the town is appointed.

We don't want to have a government that guarantees liberty and justice only for wealthy people, those who can afford an attorney. We want liberty and justice for all people.

Habeas Corpus

Habeus Corpus means, "You should have the body," in Latin. A person arrested for a crime has the right to know the body of proof or evidence (probable cause) that is being used against him. This can be obtained by submitting a *Writ of Habeas Corpus* to the court. If this process shows that the person has been held without sufficient legal cause, he may be released.

Bail

Bail is money or other security (something of value) given to secure a person's release from custody. Bail is often set at a large amount, to assure the court that if they let the defendant go free before the trial, he or she would most certainly appear in court on the trial date.

When bail is discussed with the judge, he or she considers the charge and thinks about whether the defendant is a good risk. If the judge does not think the defendant is dependable, the judge can deny bail, or can set bail at such a huge amount of money that the defendant can't get that amount and must stay in custody. The Eighth Amendment to the Constitution guarantees your right against unreasonable bail. This can be tricky, because to some very poor people even fifty dollars might be unreasonable.

A bail bond is an official paper signed by the accused to insure his presence at the trial. The accused is technically under arrest and under the power of the justice system, but after posting bail he may remain free during the wait for the trial. There may be certain restrictions, but the defendant can continue work and live at home until and during the trial.

Most people do not have huge amounts of money available. If they are arrested and need bail money, they can go to a bail bond office to borrow the money. The bondsman will post the bail for the accused if he thinks the accused is a good risk. For lending this money the bondsman charges a fee. If the defendant appears at the trial, the bond money is returned to the bondsman. If the defendant runs away or hides, if he breaks the promise to appear for trial, the bail is forfeited (not returned), and a bulletin is issued for his arrest. The bondsman will also send people to find him. The bondsman does not like to lose money, and he will be very angry at the defendant.

Chapter 12
THE RIGHT TO A TRIAL

The newspaper reported that a trial was held in Baghdad, Iraq. The defendant was present but he was not represented by an attorney. There were no witnesses, no evidence. The door to the courtroom was locked. There were no reporters and no observers. In fifteen minutes the "trial" was over. The defendant was found guilty. Was this justice?

In the United States, a trial is usually held in a courtroom. It is a situation where both sides of the legal argument have a chance to present what they think they can prove to a jury or a judge. There are two major types of trials, civil trials and criminal trials. We have already discussed the difference between civil law and criminal law, but let's take a closer look at what this difference means at the time of a trial.

Civil Trial

A civil trial is held when one person (or company) sues another for a legal decision to settle a dispute, when it does not involve breaking the law. An action that involves a private civil wrong—either by doing something or not doing something—is called a *tort* rather than a *crime*. A civil trial can be decided by a judge or a jury. The defendant can say which he or she wants. That kind of trial involves civil law.

If a person feels that he has suffered because of the actions of another, he can sue that person. To start a civil suit, the person starting the action works with an attorney. They submit a written statement explaining their action. This is called the *complaint*. The person starting the lawsuit is the *plaintiff*.

The person being sued is the *defendant*. He and his attorney answer the complaint by submitting a written report denying or accepting the charge. This is called the *answer*. If the defendant does not file an answer he will be considered *at fault* (guilty) and must pay or satisfy the plaintiff.

At the trial, a jury usually decides the *questions in fact*. The judge decides *questions of law*. If both sides wish, the judge alone may decide the questions of fact and law.

By listening to both sides, the jury and the judge can see where the differences of opinion lie. Both sides produce evidence, which may be physical, written, or attested to (sworn to) by witnesses. After all the evidence is in, the judge tells the jury about the rules of law in the case. Then the jury deliberates (discusses the evidence) and decides for which side they *find* (who wins). The jury's decision is called the verdict. If the charge was proved, the jury can also decide how much money the plaintiff will win. This verdict is given to the judge, who makes his judgment in relationship to the verdict.

That is how a civil case proceeds.

Criminal Trial

A criminal trial is held when a person has allegedly broken a law and is prosecuted by "the people." The people are represented by someone from the district attorney's office. For serious crimes that have been proved in court, there may be a separate sentencing trial with a jury to determine the punishment, as in a murder trial with the possibilities of life in prison or execution. A criminal trial involves public law.

The person who is on trial is the *defendant*. The person representing the people is the *prosecutor*, and usually is from the district attorney's office. Because the Constitution assures that a person is considered innocent until proved guilty, the prosecutor must present a case that proves the charge through evidence and the testimony of witnesses. The "burden of proof" is the responsibility of the prosecution, not the defendant, as we have said before.

The Fifth Amendment to the Constitution assures us that a person cannot be tried twice for the same charge if he or she was found not guilty the first time. This would be called *double jeopardy*, and refers to criminal trials only. Sometimes there can be a second trial if the verdict was guilty and someone wants to bring a civil suit.

Types of Courts and Levels of Courts

Courts were established to give people a chance to be heard in an impartial way that conforms to the Constitution and its guarantees. A court is a government agency with the power to settle disputes between individuals and organizations. The word *court* may mean the place where judges and other persons meet to settle legal disputes, or it may mean the "gathering" itself.

The court systems of the United States are based on that of England, so let's review a bit. During the eleventh and twelfth centuries in England, the king and a group of officials and noblemen traveled about the country, hearing complaints and criminal charges. The officials who followed the king were called his *court*. The king was thought of as the supreme source of justice, but he couldn't be everywhere. So, he established a system of central courts and appointed officers to hear cases and administer justice for him. These men were the early judges.

While America still belonged to England, provincial courts were set up in each of the thirteen colonies. After the Revolutionary War in America, each state set up a court system modeled after English courts.

The Constitution provides that:

> "The judicial power of the United States shall be vested in one Supreme Court, and in such inferior courts as the Congress may from time to time ordain and establish."

Most states have a constitution, a supreme court, and many lower courts. State courts handle domestic affairs, those cases that involve state laws and regulations. The federal courts handle disputes between people from different states that involve federal law, U.S. constitutional law, and international law.

Federal Court System

The highest court of the United States is the U.S. Supreme Court. It has the power of *judicial review*. That means it can declare whether any law that is challenged is constitutional or unconstitutional. The Supreme Court can declare unconstitutional an executive order (an order from the president), legislative acts (laws made by Congress), or any law or act of the federal and state governments.

The U.S. Supreme Court has the power to rule on questions of interpreting the U.S. Constitution. Whenever the highest court in one state decides a question on the meaning of the U.S. Constitution, the U.S. Supreme Court can review that decision and confirm or overrule it. When a lower court case has been decided by interpreting the Constitution, an unsuccessful plaintiff or defendant may ask for a review. The formal request is called a *writ of certiorari*.

The federal judicial system is rather simple. There is at least one U.S. district court in each of the fifty states. These courts are called *courts of general jurisdiction*. They have the power to hear and pass judgment on both civil and criminal cases including cases that involve violations of your personal civil rights and cases involving violation of federal criminal laws.

In federal district court civil cases there are two restrictions. The plaintiff and defendant must each live in different states, and the amount involved in the lawsuit must be over $10,000. That is a great deal more money than was stated originally in the Seventh Amendment, where the amount was set at twenty dollars. Times have changed!

Federal courts may try certain lawsuits that do not depend on where the defendant and plaintiff came from, or the amount of money involved. Some cases belong to the federal courts because the Constitution says so, or because Congress has said so. Among these are bankruptcy, patents, trademarks, copyrights, and admiralty matters.

State and Local Courts

State courts are much like federal courts in methods of procedure and in their powers, though they differ widely from state to state. (When I explain courtroom procedures in Chapter 13, I will describe a system like those found in a majority of states.)

In a state, the highest court is the state supreme court, which hears appeals from all lower courts. It is a court of last appeal unless the case involves constitutional matters at which point it could go to the U.S. Supreme Court.

A trial court, also often called *superior court*, hears felony criminal cases and civil cases involving $25,000 or more. Trial courts also hear domestic, juvenile delinquency, and youthful offender cases. These cases usually are under the juvenile or family court division.

Trial courts include municipal or state district courts in large areas, which may hear less serious civil and criminal cases. A municipal court has jurisdiction over civil actions involving $25,000 or less, small claims involving $5,000 or less, criminal infractions (violations for which the punishment is a fine, not jail time), and crimes that are not a felony.

In smaller areas there are local courts which are called by different names. Justice courts are established where there are fewer than 40,000 people. These courts have jurisdiction over small claims up to $500 and action at law up to $1,000. Some villages have a justice of the peace, a magistrate's court, a traffic court, a police court, or a small claims court. If a person wants the case to be heard by a higher court, he or she has that right. Or the case may be heard by the lower court and the defendant may take an appeal to the next higher court.

Courts Can Bring about Changes in the Law

Courts do not make laws, but they can interpret and reinterpret existing ones in ways that can completely change old, established laws or customs. As we saw in earlier chapters, laws that worked well a hundred years ago might not apply today without some rethinking. For example, the courts are being asked to re-evaluate the Second Amendment to the Constitution, which deals with a person's right to bear arms (to carry guns everywhere). During the early days, carrying a gun was important for a person's safety since there were not many policemen or sheriffs. People also had to hunt for their food and protect themselves from wild animals. But our customs and needs are different now. Many people are calling for a "gun control" measure on the ballot. Others are asking for a change of the Second Amendment, which would involve a Supreme Court ruling. It is a very hot debate, with good points on both sides. Some day you may be asked to vote on this. It is important that you keep informed and important that you vote.

The District Attorney (the Prosecution)

Here are the facts of a case. You are the district attorney. A report is given to you. You decide what will happen.

"Suspect was observed entering the said premises about one forty-five p.m. According to witnesses they observed motion in the house, but reported hearing no noise. Suspect was not observed leaving the house.

Victims returned to find the place a mess and things missing. Victims called 911 and requested police action. Officers arrived at the house at three o'clock that same afternoon. Officers searched the premises. Suspect was found sleeping in one of the bedrooms. Suspect was cooperative and submitted to arrest. Suspect was transferred to the police station for identification and questioning.

The detective detail went through the house and reported the home had not been locked. Suspect did not break in, but entered the premises freely. The house was in disarray. Furniture was broken, dishes were broken, food had been eaten, and belongings had been taken or moved."

Suppose you are with the justice system. How will you work on this case? First, imagine that you are the police officer. How will you charge the suspect? Breaking and entering? Burglary? Vandalism? Robbery? Now pretend you are the district attorney. With what charge will you send this case to arraignment? Or will you press charges at all? If this case goes to trial, suppose you are the defense attorney. How will you advise your client? What will you tell the jury? You may have heard of this case before! Check it out when you reach the end of the chapter.

The district attorney's office is the agency that makes the decision whether to prosecute. It has the power to:

- File charges

- Conduct investigations

- Bring evidence to a grand jury

- Prosecute the case in trial

- Dismiss the case or charges.

When a crime has been committed and a suspect is arrested, a large amount of paperwork is started. The police file a report of the incident. Investigators file reports of their findings. Charges against the suspect are filed. Any probation or parole reports are included if the suspect has a previous criminal record. In most law enforcement agencies, an officer is assigned the duty of carrying each day's reports by hand to the district attorney's office.

In some states, a deputy district attorney is assigned to review the case. (Other communities call him or her an *intake deputy* or a *supervising deputy.*) This is one of the most important jobs in the office. The deputy decides who will be prosecuted, under what charges, and who might not be charged (perhaps because he or she is wanted as a witness). Five to ten percent of all cases are rejected by the district attorney for lack of information.

Many cases are dismissed, but most end in conviction because of plea bargaining. This is explained further on in this chapter. For this reason, the district attorney affects most of the sentencing in many areas. It means he can offer the defendant a lighter sentence if he will plead guilty instead of going to trial. The lighter sentence is presented to the judge as a recommendation from the district attorney's office. Most judges follow these recommendations.

The prosecution bears the "burden of proof" (remember— that means they must prove the charge and the defendant does not have to prove himself or herself innocent). To prove the charge, the district attorney has much help. He or she can use the detective bureau, police reports, the crime lab for evidence. The district attorney will gather (subpoena) witnesses who can testify about the defendant or the crime. (A *subpoena* is a legal demand that the person to whom it is issued must appear at the time requested.)

The Defense Attorney and the Public Defender's Office

The nation saw it on television. Over and over the news showed pictures of John Hinkley shooting President Reagan. Hinkley was arrested and pled not guilty. At the trial his attorney defended him by trying to prove that he was not guilty by reason of insanity. That is exactly what the jury decided.

The verdict troubled many people. They had all seen the shooting on television. Mr. Hinkley was observed by witnesses. "How could anyone defend him?" they asked. "Why waste money on a trial?" Does everyone deserve a defense?

Indeed, even the person who is seen committing the most terrible acts must have all the benefits of our justice system. If that system really works, the defendant will be given a just verdict—and if found guilty, a just punishment. We must never be so bloodthirsty for revenge that we destroy the basis of our entire justice system. If once in a while a guilty person "gets away" without paying his debt to society, so be it. Revenge could blind us to the higher ideal. All accused persons have a right to a defense—the best defense our government can provide, whether they can pay for it or not.

Our justice system has public defender's offices throughout the land. Many very good lawyers work there. It is their job to see that a suspect who cannot afford to hire an attorney is given the best legal advice and the best defense possible. This is guaranteed under the Sixth Amendment to the Constitution.

Even though the Constitution assures the defendant that he is considered innocent until proved guilty, the defendant needs an attorney to make sure that everything done to him, for him, or with him, is in his best legal interest. The defense attorney might want to present a defense just to make sure the jury gets all the best information about the defendant.

As mentioned before, the defense attorney works with the defendant to prepare for the arraignment. Together they decide how the defendant will answer the charge. In preparation for a trial, the defense attorney prepares a *defense* that will help his or her client. Even though presumed innocent, the defendant was arrested because the evidence showed *probable cause*. The district attorney (prosecutor) will use that evidence to try to prove the defendant guilty.

Since the burden of proof is on the prosecutor, the defense attorney does not have to present any defense at all. Legally he or she could sit back and say, "Prove it!" But the defense attorney does not sit back. It is very important to check on all witnesses, all evidence, all the "proof" the district attorney will be presenting.

The defense attorney must see that everything in the trial and the pretrial process is legal and in the best interest of the client. If the defendant can speak well and tell what happened, if he has some witnesses who will say he didn't commit the crime—couldn't possibly have committed the crime—then his attorney will, of course, present a defense. The defense might also find expert witnesses to prove the defendant is innocent, or perhaps to argue against any expert witnesses the prosecution might present. Even though the defense attorney does not have to prove his client not guilty, he wants very much to plant some doubt in the jury's minds. Remember that the judge will tell the jury that if they find the defendant guilty, they must do so beyond a reasonable doubt.

The defense has access to all the lab reports and other evidence that the prosecution will enter for the trial, and must be informed of all the witnesses to be called. The defense can also hire private detectives and experts and has the legal right and power, guaranteed in the Sixth Amendment, to subpoena witnesses. (The prosecution also has rights to any information the defense has gathered.)

Getting Ready for a Criminal Trial

It costs thousands of dollars to prosecute a crime and conduct a trial, and court calendars are very crowded, so the government makes quite sure it has a strong case before it goes to the trouble and expense of a trial. We should feel grateful to have law enforcement officers to take criminals off the streets, and we are equally lucky to have people in the justice system to make fair trials possible.

Investigation and Evidence

Many processes have to happen after a defendant pleads not guilty. As we have seen, the district attorney's office has to decide if they want to "go to trial" with the case. They must investigate and gather evidence. They must decide if they have enough evidence to prove the defendant guilty beyond a reasonable doubt. The prosecution has to present the case at an arraignment. If the case involves a felony, the case will be presented at a preliminary hearing or a grand jury hearing.

In a criminal trial, only the prosecution *must* produce evidence and witnesses in order to prove the case against the defendant. If the defense wants to present evidence and witnesses it certainly may during the defense phase of the trial.

Level of Crime

Cases are filed as infractions, misdemeanors, or felonies. The possible punishment depends on the level of the crime. For an infraction like a speeding ticket, you do not go to jail, but only have to pay a fine. For conviction of a misdemeanor, you can go to county jail, as well as pay a fine. For a felony, you can be sent to state or federal prison. For murder, you can even be executed.

Arraignments and Hearings before the Trial

In states like California, which have a grand jury system, a case can go directly to superior court for trial after a grand jury indictment (accusation). Further on in this chapter there is a section explaining the grand jury process. But first let's look at the more usual procedure after an arrest.

Most cases go to a lower court, such as a municipal court, for arraignment. If the case is filed as a felony and the defendant's plea is "not guilty," a preliminary hearing is held within ten days to have a judge decide if there is enough evidence (*probable cause*) to convict the defendant. The judge must decide two things:

1. Is there enough evidence to prove that a crime was committed?

2. Is the defendant the one who probably committed the crime?

If satisfied that the answers are "yes," the judge then says, "I hold the defendant to answer as charged. I certify this case to Superior Court." A second arraignment is then held in Superior Court. An accusatory pleading has to be filed within fifteen days. After that, a readiness and settlement hearing is held with the defendant and the attorneys present. If the attorneys decide not to go to trial they will work out a settlement at that time. If they decide not to settle, a date will be set for a jury trial.

Plea Bargains

The district attorney's office and the public defender's office (or other defense attorney) can arrange plea bargains. Overcrowding in the courts is a big problem. There is a huge backlog of cases waiting to be heard. We simply do not have enough court time and jail space to try each case. Therefore plea bargaining is a fact of life. In a plea bargain, the defendant may plead guilty in return for being charged with a less serious offense. Defense attorneys usually urge their clients to plead guilty if the evidence strongly indicates the defendant's guilt.

Here's an example. In preparing a charge against a defendant, the district attorney wants to charge the suspect with Murder 1 (murder in the first degree), but looking at the evidence it seems that this would very difficult to prove. The district attorney might work out a deal with the defendant and his or her attorney to lower the charge to Murder 2, which has a lesser sentence. The defendant agrees to plead guilty and a trial is not needed. The district attorney's recommendation for the charge and sentencing are presented to the judge. Most judges follow these recommendations.

In many misdemeanor cases where the defendant pleads not guilty, the case goes to a readiness and settlement conference instead of to a court trial. Here both attorneys talk about the facts of the case, possible defenses, the defendant's prior record, and any other information that is important to the case. Together they work toward some solution that will satisfy the court. This information is presented to the judge, who then hands down the sentence based on these recommendations.

The Grand Jury

Sometimes a felony suspect is not arrested, arraigned, and brought to trial in the way I have been describing. Some communities use a group of citizens called a *grand jury* to decide if a felony case has enough probable cause to go to trial. It is usually the district attorney's office that presents the case to the grand jury. The procedure is called a *grand jury hearing*. "Hearsay" evidence is allowed. That means that police officers and other witnesses can testify to what all parties said about what happened. (In front of a regular trial jury, witnesses can only tell what they know personally.)

When a grand jury *indicts* (formally charges) a defendant, the case goes right to superior court for trial. It does not go through the lower courts at all. This saves many dollars for the government because there is no need for a preliminary hearing, as there would be otherwise after an arraignment on a felony charge.

The district attorney shows the grand jury that a crime was committed. by presenting a *prima facie* case. This means sufficient evidence to establish that there is a case against the accused. The district attorney then asks for a *true bill*, an indictment from the grand jury. If convinced, the grand jury formally indicts (accuses) the defendant. This is called an *accusatory pleading*. The defendant and defense attorney then find out about the charges, perhaps for the first time. They do not have to be told in advance.

As the Time for Trial Approaches

If the defendant is held without bail for a long time before the trial, a problem arises. The person was arrested and held for probable cause, but he or she is still presumed innocent until proved guilty. A long time in jail before trial is hard to justify. The Constitution assures us a speedy trial. If the defendant is later found not guilty, we must feel troubled about the time spent in jail. There is another side to this question, though. In certain cases this delay or a long trial can be to the defendant's advantage. Memory fades as time passes, and it is difficult to get witnesses to testify with hard facts two years later.

The scheduling of a trial depends partly on the seriousness of the crime and what is needed to prepare the case. The trial for a misdemeanor case may be scheduled at the time of arraignment. For a more serious or complex case, there might be more delay. Witnesses must be called, evidence must be collected, and the defense must be ready to participate. A time must also be found on the court calendar.

Most American courts are crowded. For most felonies, attorneys must wait for their case to be scheduled on the master court calendar. Murder cases take about a year to come to trial. The master calendar is prepared by a clerk of the court who receives a list of cases and the name of the judges assigned by the presiding judge. One judge is chosen each year to be presiding judge. He or she assigns cases, presides over indictments. The presiding judge also holds readiness and settlement sessions and other legal hearings that come before a trial. He or she usually does not have time to do regular trial work during that year.

When the trial has been scheduled, the attorneys are advised of the date. Time limits are set by law so that cases are finished in a reasonable time. Before the time set for the trial, the attorneys for both sides meet with the judge to discuss the case. In outlining their cases to the judge, the defense and prosecution both must reveal their information and the witnesses they plan to call. If one attorney is surprised during the trial by what is brought before the court, the other attorney can get a one-day *continuance* (a one-day delay) to study and prepare to respond to this surprise. Or he or she can *move* (ask) that the evidence not be allowed to be used.

What's Next?

Now that we've talked about all the work that goes into getting ready for a trial, and the different kinds of courts and trials, at last it is time to turn to the trial itself. What happens during a criminal trial? Who are the people who play a part in the trial? That's that the next chapter is about.

By the way, the case presented on pages 76 and 77 was an old story you might have recognized. The defendant was Goldilocks!

Chapter 13
WHAT HAPPENS AT A TRIAL

The Courtroom

For a trial the courtroom is usually set up as shown in the diagram on the next page.

The People Who Work in the Courtroom

There are many people who play a part in a trial. (Members of the public may also be present to observe.) In the Activities and Games at the end of this book, I have included a section called "Judge for Yourself." It presents little scenes or scenarios of problems which could require the help of people in the legal justice system. It might be fun for you to go through the section taking the roles of some of the court personnel. In addition to the defendant, here are the other main participants in a trial.

The Judge

The judge is an attorney who has been practicing law for at least ten years and has been appointed or elected to the position. There are judges at all levels of the court system. It is the duty of the judge to control all proceedings during a trial. This duty includes limiting the introduction of evidence and the arguments of attorneys to "relevant and material" matters that have to do only with the trial. The judge instructs the jury and acts upon the jury's findings.

There are judges of the Justice Court, the Municipal Court, the Superior Court, and/or the Supreme Court of each state. There are also judges in the federal court system, including

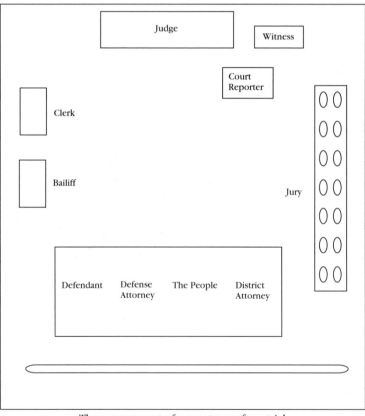

The arrangement of a courtroom for a trial.

the District Court, the Court of Appeals, the U.S. Supreme Court, and various specialized courts.

The Jury

The jury is a group of citizens chosen from a list of registered voters and other lists such as Department of Motor Vehicles records. They are called (subpoenaed) to do jury duty. They are required by law to appear and be ready to sit through this trial and vote their decision.

To be released from jury duty, a person must prove to the judge that he or she is unable to serve. This could be for a health reason, some personal problem, or hardship. It is not an excuse that you would miss work, for an employer is forbidden to punish a worker for missing work because of jury duty. If a person is self-employed and it would be a hardship to stop working and miss being paid, or to close down a business, the person might be excused. Women with young children also might find it a hardship to leave home to serve and are usually excused. Jurors are paid a small sum for serving.

The prospective jurors (persons on a jury panel) are questioned by both attorneys in a process called *voir dire* (a French expression meaning to see and speak). The attorneys are allowed to excuse a certain number of jurors they do not want to "sit" on this particular trial. For example, in a trial involving a banker, an attorney might not want a certain juror who said he once had very serious trouble with a banker. Or if a prospective juror said that she had lost much money in the stock market, and the trial involved a stock investment, she would probably be excused from serving. One of the attorneys might excuse a juror to balance the group if the jury seemed to be all women or all men, or if most of the jury was of one race or color. It is most desirable for a jury to represent a wide range of people with different educational levels and interests. That is why it is important that everyone serves.

Often people who are busy in professional jobs feel that they cannot give the time to be on a jury, so they try very hard to get off. And yet these same people, if they were on trial, would want a jury of intelligent, active citizens judging them. We do not want juries made up of only people with nothing else to do. They can be good and valuable citizens, but we want a good mixture of people, a broad cross-section of our society.

Alternate jurors are chosen in case a regular juror cannot serve through the whole trial. If a juror became ill or had an emergency—or if the juror did not obey the judge and broke one of the rules, that juror would be *excused* (taken off the jury) and the alternate would take his place. For trials that are expected to last a long time, two or more alternates are chosen. They "sit" throughout the trial and are treated the same as jurors so they can take over if needed. If the regular jurors complete the trial, the alternates are excused.

Trial procedures in regard to juries vary from state to state. In Arkansas it takes only nine out of twelve people on a jury to reach a decision. Most states require a unanimous verdict (for which everyone must agree), especially in criminal cases. In some states, civil cases and misdemeanors may be tried in lower courts before a six-person jury.

After the jurors are chosen they are sworn in by the court clerk, and the record shows that the "jurors are seated." At this point if a juror does not obey what the judge says, he or she can be arrested. This only happens in rare cases where a juror perhaps takes a bribe or disregards the instructions of the judge.

Lawyers

Lawyers, also called attorneys, appear in court to represent their clients. We have mentioned prosecutors from the district attorney's office and defense attorneys from the public defender's office and from private practice. We have also read about attorneys who do not do criminal law, but bring civil complaints on behalf of their clients.

Lawyers work on hundreds of other legal proceedings in and out of court besides trials, such as filing papers to start businesses, attending to wills, registering property, adopting children, getting a divorce, filing for bankruptcy, and many other matters. These proceedings are usually conducted with attorneys representing their clients.

An attorney may attend law school or "read the law" (this means independent study). It is not enough just to graduate from law school or have a law degree. In order to practice law, to take on clients and use the courts for their clients, a lawyer must pass a very difficult test called the *bar examination*. Only upon passing the "bar" is an attorney admitted to the practice of law. Each state has its own rules and its own bar exam. Some examinations are more difficult than others. A lawyer cannot practice law in another state unless he or she qualifies by passing the bar of that state or fulfilling certain requirements.

The Bailiff

The bailiff is a member of the sheriff's or marshal's office. The bailiff may be from other departments in different states, but the duties are basically the same all over. This deputy is assigned to court and works for a particular judge. The bailiff's responsibility is to take charge of the defendant, to take charge of the jury, to keep order in the courtroom, and to summon witnesses when they are called.

The Clerk

The clerk is a very important member of the trial team. The clerk swears in all witnesses, swears in the jury, and enters the evidence in the trial log. He or she swears in the bailiff when the bailiff takes charge of the jury before deliberation. The clerk accepts the jury's finding and announces it to the court.

The Court Reporter

The court reporter records every word of testimony or legal conversation that occurs during the trial. The court reporter also takes depositions (written testimony under oath) before the trial and records conversations of the judge and lawyer that should be in the legal record.

Witnesses

There are witnesses in a trial if either attorney has subpoenaed any (called by a legal demand that they appear). A witness is someone who answers questions and tells facts (testifies) to the jury while under oath (having sworn to tell the truth). An eyewitness testifies to what he has experienced by his presence at an event. For example, if a witness saw the defendant in Santa Barbara at eight p.m. on Saturday night, July 4, 1992, and the crime was committed in another city on that night, the defense would certainly want that witness to testify before the jury. This would be proof that the defendant could not have committed the crime, since he couldn't be in two places at one time.

A character witness is someone who knows the defendant and can tell things that will help the jury to know what kind of person the defendant is. Some character witnesses might say the defendant is someone who is a good student, someone who goes to church, works hard, and does many good things for people in the town. What would you think if a character witness said that he had known the defendant for years and that the defendant was always getting into trouble, was always fighting, was caught stealing, and did mean things? Which attorney do you think would call that man to be a witness? I am sure that the prosecutor would want the jury to hear those unpleasant things about the defendant. But—character witnesses may only tell about the parts of the defendant's character that have to do with the crime charged or the reliability of the defendant as a witness. "Always fighting" would not relate to the crime of drunk driving. "Lying" would not relate to the crime of robbery.

An expert witness can be called by either attorney to help explain things to the judge or jury. For instance, if the attorneys want to present any scientific information, they might have a scientist with special knowledge testify. Remember that the prosecutor has the crime lab to help prove the charge against the defendant. The crime lab often sends expert witnesses to talk about blood samples, alcohol testing, fingerprints, gun testing, and so on. Other expert witnesses from outside the justice system are often paid for appearing. Expert witnesses may state opinions, while other witnesses must only state facts and are not allowed to tell what they think.

There is another kind of witness who does not appear for either side, but volunteers to offer information on the law or the facts of the case. Such a witness is called a Latin name, *amicus curiae* (friend of the court).

Sometimes it is necessary to call children as witnesses. If they are very young, the reliability of their testimony may be doubtful. Here is a story about such a case.

> It was a case that inflamed the nation. It was one of the first times that a preschool operator was accused of molesting a child—in fact, many children. The newspaper and television covered it sensationally. The children involved were relating incredible stories.
>
> As the district attorney prepared his case, the stories grew. The children were questioned over and over by their parents, the police, the lawyers, neighbors, and friends. These children were very young, between two and five years old. Because of their age, most of the questions were in the form of statements to which the children only had to answer "yes" or "no." For many months the children heard these statements over and over. You can see why it was hard for them to tell the difference between what really happened and what they were told happened.

Two years later the trial finally began. Two years is a long time to remember accurately, especially if you are very young. Also, the children were not cross-examined, but their statements were admitted as testimony. They were too young to be legal witnesses, yet the entire case depended on what they said because they were the alleged victims and only they and the operators of the school were directly involved.

In many states a witness must be at least ten years old and must be able to *observe, recall,* and *relate*. In other states the age isn't specified, but the judge determines if the child is competent (able) to testify. When anyone is a witness he or she must understand what it means to legally swear to tell the truth.

It doesn't matter what the witness thinks, it only matters what he saw and heard. If he saw a crime happen, the more he saw the better. That is called *observing.*

When a witness is asked to *recall,* it means he or she must remember accurately. Perhaps the question will be about something that happened months ago. Perhaps the attorney wants to know the time a certain action happened, or the color of a person's shirt, or the kind of car he was driving. When a person's freedom or life is at stake, it is very important to be really sure. A witness must not just say things because he or she feels important with everyone paying attention.

When a witness is asked to *relate,* it means that he must tell what he observed. What he says must be accurate, truthful, and easy to understand by the jury and the judge. Both attorneys want good witnesses to help them present their cases.

It is not easy to be a good, accurate witness. In the Activities and Games part of this book there is a section called "Being a Witness" with more information about witnesses, and some games and exercises you might enjoy.

Interpreters

An interpreter is used if a defendant or witness does not speak or understand English. Trial interpreters translate each word spoken exactly as it is said—they do not *interpret*, which would mean telling in their own words what is going on. Yet, the term *interpreters* is still used.

Evidence

> Marsha was found guilty of murdering her lover and his friend. She is in prison serving two concurrent (both together) life sentences. The murder weapon was never found. It was a gun which many people saw, but suddenly it disappeared before the police could examine it. The district attorney accused Marsha's lawyer, Mr. Roberts, of "destroying the evidence," and charged him with a felony. That gun was evidence.

Let's talk about legal evidence. The dictionary tells us, "Evidence is something legally presented before a court such as a statement of a witness, or an object which tends to prove something." It makes things *evident*. It makes them clear. It makes or "establishes" a fact or a point in question.

There are rules about obtaining evidence. The Fourth Amendment of the Constitution states very clearly:

> "The right of the people to be secure in their persons, houses, papers, and effects, against unreasonable searches and seizures, shall not be violated, and no warrants shall issue, but upon probable cause, supported by oath or affirmation, and particularly describing the place to be searched, and the persons or things to be seized."

All of this means that an officer can stop and question anyone he or she has probable cause to suspect of committing a crime. Witnesses can also be questioned. But, officers must have a warrant to search and seize except in special circumstances. One such special case would be if the officer suspects a person of being under the influence of drugs. The officer can stop that person and examine for evidence of drug use. If the officer took the time to get a search warrant, the effects of the drug might wear off. That would make it impossible to prove drug use. An officer who sees or suspects that a crime is happening can search and seize without a warrant—but he or she must be sure there is probable cause. A person on probation or parole can be searched at any time if this is a condition of the probation or parole.

Earlier we said that if an officer is looking for evidence in a home, he or she must get a search warrant based on probable cause. "Probable cause" is established by evidence an officer can offer to the judge to justify the issuing of a warrant. The warrant limits the search to a certain place and describes the person or things to be seized, as required by the Fourth Amendment. In some countries, police raid homes and businesses, dragging away anyone they want. Often these people are thrown in cells and never get a trial or hearing. They do not have a constitution that protects them.

One last fact about evidence. There is a difference between direct evidence and circumstantial evidence, which can be important in trial arguments. *Direct evidence* is an eyewitness account of what was seen. Not what the witness thinks, but only fact, what the witness actually saw.

Circumstantial evidence provides information that tends to confirm or deny a fact "at issue." For example, if a defendant testifies that he absolutely did not come near the victim, but detectives find pieces of fabric from his clothing and hair from his body and his type of blood on the victim's body, this is evidence that conflicts with the defendant's testimony. It is circumstantial evidence. It makes it reasonable to infer that the defendant is not telling the truth. The crime lab is a frequent source of circumstantial evidence.

Trial Procedures

Pretrial Motions

As I mentioned before, a criminal trial usually starts with the judge meeting with both lawyers and outlining how the trial will proceed. They agree on the charges against the defendant and how the jury will be charged (instructed). These are *pretrial motions*.

At this time a process called *discovery* also takes place. This means that one party gains information concerning the case that is held by the opposing party. For example, the district attorney can demand a document, deposition, chart, or other evidence held by the defense, and likewise the defense can demand evidence held by the district attorney. Discovery is part of the pretrial motions.

Jury Selection

Now the job of jury selection begins. The judge usually talks with prospective jurors and tells them a little of what the trial is about. He or she asks if anyone thinks they cannot serve. Following that, the judge and maybe the attorneys begin questioning the people one by one. As many as fifty or sixty persons might be questioned before twelve jurors and two alternates are selected. Many courts now have prospective jurors fill out a questionnaire to be read by the attorneys and the judge, which saves time. The intention of jury selection is to choose jurors who can be fair in a particular case.

The Trial Begins

After all the jurors are chosen, the actual trial begins. The bailiff calls the court to order and the judge is seated. The judge announces the name of the case and asks the clerk to swear in the jurors. When this is done, the judge asks both attorneys for opening statements.

An opening statement is a short talk each attorney makes to the jury telling them what the trial is about. The prosecutor usually tells them the charges made against the defendant and explains how he or she intends to prove the defendant is guilty. The defense attorney usually tells the jury that the defendant is not guilty and how he or she plans to show it.

The Attorneys Present Their Cases

Following the opening statements, the judge usually tells the prosecutor to call his or her first witness. The prosecutor is called on first because the "burden of proof" is on him or her. Remember that I told you a person is considered innocent until proved guilty. The prosecutor must prove to the jury that the defendant is guilty.

The prosecutor should be well prepared. He should know just what he wants to ask the witnesses to prove the case. The prosecutor has already gone through many questions with witnesses before the trial. By the time they are in court he knows pretty well what these witnesses will answer. He does not want any surprises.

For every fact the prosecutor wants to establish (tell the jury), he needs to present a witness or evidence to prove that fact so the jury will believe it. If he wants the jury to know about a weapon—say a gun, the prosecutor will have the person who found the gun testify. This word *testify* means that the witness will tell the jury the facts, or answer the questions, while "under oath" (having sworn to tell the truth). The witness must tell the truth and can be arrested if proved to be lying. Lying under oath is a crime called *perjury*.

There are certain rules about the way witnesses can be questioned in front of a jury. After either one of the attorneys has called and questioned a witness, the opposing attorney may also ask questions of the same witness. This is called *cross-examination*. In cross-examination, the questions must be in the "line of questioning" begun by the first attorney. That means that if one side asks a witness about the defendant as a student at school, about his grades and activities in sports, and about his family, the attorney doing the cross-examination cannot switch subjects. He cannot start to ask about whether the defendant went to jail for any other crime, or drives his car too fast.

In order to reach a point in questioning where the answer is significant, the attorney must build to that point. It is called "laying a foundation." Fact after fact is brought out leading to the obvious conclusion desired. For example, to make it clear that a witness speaks with authority, the attorney might ask him about where he lives, his education, his work, his relationship to the defendant, and so on.

If the opposing attorney wants to begin a different line of questioning, he can state that he reserves the right to recall the witness later when he presents his case. At that time, on direct examination, he can ask about almost anything he wants.

Let's return to the prosecutor now. When the prosecutor has finished presenting the case against the defendant, he states, "The prosecution rests."

That literally could end the trial, because the defense does not have to prove anything. But if the defense attorney has some good witnesses who might convince the jury to believe the defendant, it would be well for them to testify. If the defense has any scientific proof that the defendant is innocent, he would certainly want to present that. If the defense has any good character witnesses, they should be called to testify. Of course, the prosecution can cross-examine any witnesses the defense brings. The point is that the defense would like to cast doubt on all the statements and "proof" that the prosecution presents. When finished, the defense attorney states, "The defense rests."

Closing Arguments

During a trial the questions go on and on, and the witnesses come and go. A trial can take many days, weeks, months, and even years. But when the defense rests, the trial is almost over. The judge asks the attorneys if they are ready for *closing arguments*. This is an opportunity for the attorneys to have one more chance to talk to the jury. Each attorney told the jury in the opening statement that he would prove this and that. He now will tell them that he did prove these things, and will probably outline these points to make sure the jury heard what he wanted them to hear. He can also argue against anything the opposing side presented and perhaps convince the jury to disregard it.

First the prosecution presents its closing statement, followed by the defense. Then the prosecutor has one last chance to speak to the jury, because the burden of proof lies with him or her.

If Members of the Jury Have Questions

Now if you sat in court and watched a trial you might think of questions you wish the attorneys would ask. It can be very frustrating for a juror if he or she has questions, and the answers are never brought out during the trial. In some courts the judge allows the jury to submit questions and the judge will talk them over with the attorneys in private. If they agree, the judge will answer the juror's question, or allow the question to be answered by a witness.

The jury can also ask to see a transcript of the testimony obtained days or weeks ago, which was recorded by the court reporter.

The Judge Instructs the Jury

Before the jury leaves the courtroom for their deliberation, the judge speaks to them. He or she tells them that they should not talk to or listen to anyone outside of the jury about the case. The judge tells them that the only thing they can consider is what they heard in court. If the case was reported on television or in the newspaper or they heard about it from a friend or neighbor, they should still only consider the facts they heard in court. The attorneys presented the facts of the case. Witnesses and evidence were used to prove the facts.

Now the judge teaches the jury the law as it pertains to the trial. It is the job of the jury to apply the facts to the law and make a decision on the guilt or innocence of the defendant. The judge tells the jury not to judge anyone by their looks, or language, or education, or riches, or power, or color, or religion. The judge wants them to depend on their thinking, not their feelings. The defendant is to be judged only by the facts.

The judge also reminds the jurors that they must be sure *beyond a reasonable doubt*. That is an important phrase. You cannot say, "I think so." You must be able to say, "I know."

The Jury Does Its Job

After the jurors are instructed by the judge, they are taken to the jury deliberation room by the bailiff. When the bailiff takes charge of the jury, the court clerk administers an oath in which the bailiff swears to "take charge of the jury, keeping them together at all times, not allowing them to talk to you or anyone outside the jury, and to deliver the final verdict to the court."

As the jurors start their deliberation (making their judgment), they must first choose a foreman or forewoman. This person will organize their discussions and then take a vote. In some cases the first juror to be chosen becomes the foreman or forewoman.

When the jury reaches a verdict (decides whether the defendant is guilty of the charge or not), or if the jury has really tried and cannot agree, the foreman or forewoman calls the bailiff and sends that message to the courtroom. The bailiff calls the judge, the attorneys, and the defendant to assemble. The jury then returns to the courtroom. The judge asks the jurors if they have reached a *verdict* (their decision). If they answer yes, the judge calls for the verdict. The foreman or forewoman hands the written verdict to the bailiff. The bailiff shows the verdict to the judge, who silently reads it and hands it back. The bailiff then hands it over to the clerk, who records it. The verdict is then read aloud by the clerk or by the foreman or forewoman of the jury. The judge asks the members of the jury if they all agree. If that is so, the judge thanks the jury and dismisses it. If the jury reports that it cannot come to an agreement, the judge may instruct them to go back to the deliberation room and try again; or a mistrial may be declared.

Sentencing

In some cases the trial jury decides the punishment at the time of agreeing on the verdict. If a verdict of guilty is punishable in a number of ways, such as time in prison and a fine, or time in prison without a fine, or a fine without prison, the jury might be asked to decide this. But in most trials, the judge sets the sentence as the law requires.

There can be a procedure in which the jury listens to testimony from the attorneys and witnesses after the verdict, but before sentence is imposed. This is called the penalty phase. For instance, if the jury finds the defendant guilty of Murder 1, the sentence could be years in prison or life in prison or the death sentence. There might be a second trial to examine certain evidence that can help the jurors decide the punishment. At this time certain evidence may be presented that might not have been allowed during the regular trial, such as previous crimes for which the defendant might have been convicted. This is done most often in trials in which the defendant is convicted of Murder 1 and a decision must be made whether to recommend life or death.

Activities and Games

Two sections have already been mentioned that can help you learn more about what has to be considered in a trial: "Judge for Yourself," and "Being a Witness." These are found at the end of the book in the Activities and Games, along with "Fractured Fairytales," which asks you to try out your new knowledge about the law.

The Main Point

The main point of telling you about a trial is to emphasize that all persons are to be treated as equals. They are to be given the same fair treatment no matter what may be their wealth, education, or importance in the community. The guarantees of the Constitution are upheld assuring the rights of all people, and this is most important throughout our legal system.

Chapter 14
JUVENILE JUSTICE

Janie is a nice kid. She has never been in trouble with the law. Janie is a bit shy and has trouble making friends; she wants so very much to be popular. Patty asks Janie if she would like to be one of the "D-Jays" at school. Great! thinks Janie. This is a real "in" group, and they help each other. Some of them are cheerleaders, and that means games and trips. Patty tells Janie that some of the girls formed a kind of inner club, and the next meeting will be on Saturday in the mall. It is sort of an initiation. They just want to make sure that Janie is "cool."

At the mall, Janie meets the other girls and they sit around drinking cokes and talking. Finally, Janie is sent off to "prove herself." She must shoplift—steal just some little thing in the teen department. The others will stand around and watch.

Janie is in a panic. She has never done anything like this—ever. The girls giggle and tell her they do it all the time. "It's just a game," they tell her. "It doesn't mean anything. It isn't like the store loses anything." They all encouraged her. "The stores are all insured, you know. It's really exciting!"

Maybe you can guess the end of this story. Actually, it is just the beginning of a much larger, longer, and more serious story. That story begins, "Miss, come with me

> please. We have something to talk about. I am the store detective."

Children have rights, but they also have responsibilities. They have the responsibility to obey the law. Throughout this book, we talk about *rights,* and of course we mean the rights of people. Children are indeed people. But children are not just very short adults, they are different. Children are thought about in special ways when we discuss their needs, their rights, and the law. The law considers *all* children as juveniles (not just those who are in trouble).

When we talk of *juveniles* or *minors* we usually mean people under the age of eighteen. The exact age varies from state to state. In New York it is under the age of seventeen. In many states it is under the age of sixteen. In states where a person becomes a legal adult at sixteen, older teenagers can be tried in an adult criminal court, but if convicted, they are sentenced as *youthful offenders* rather than as criminals.

How the Juvenile Justice System Began

To begin looking at children and the law, let's start with a little history. Special rights for children are not mentioned in the Constitution. Children's rights have not always been protected as they are today. In the early years of our country, children were tried as adults. They sometimes served long prison terms in the same jails as adults. There were even some cases where children were tortured or executed.

In 1825, the New York House of Refuge was created by Quaker reformers to offer food, shelter, and education to the homeless and destitute children of New York and to remove juvenile offenders from the prison company of adult convicts.

As society began to question how juvenile problems were treated, the focus changed. Instead of only paying attention to what offenses the child had committed, the government began to think how to help any children who might become a

problem for the community. Although the idea was that children should be "treated" instead of punished, the emphasis
was still on discipline and submission (doing whatever the
adult told the minor to do). Minors who were sent to "shel-
ters" (special homes or reform schools) were kept under
strict rules and severe discipline. Some of these places were
very bad. The rigid system kept the youngsters under control,
but did not help them to try for a better life.

In 1899, the Illinois Court Act tried to improve the places
where juveniles in trouble were sent to live. Other states
tried to better their system of juvenile care, but problems
continued to exist.

Reform had to come at the federal level, and because of
public outcry it did. The result was the adoption of juvenile
justice systems throughout the United States. This reform did
not only focus on the facilities where juveniles were placed.
Attention also turned to government control over an entire
range of youthful activities that had been ignored or dealt
with informally. It is important to remember that juvenile
problems are not just crime-related problems. The welfare of
children was recognized as important, and people started to
think of society's duty to insure the rights of children.

In 1903, California was the seventh state to pass a juvenile
court act. It provided for separate court jurisdiction and hearings for dependent and delinquent children under the age of
sixteen. Under this act the juvenile court was made part of
the jurisdiction (area of authority) of the superior courts. A
change of attitude made it clear that juvenile courts were
places to help, not punish. Trained social workers were to
give the judge information on the child's personal background
and criminal history, if any. Parole officers were to study the
child's legal history and make recommendations to the judge
about the terms of any judgment that would be handed down.

For a long time the system seemed to go along smoothly. To
protect the children, juvenile courts were not open to the
public. The records on the case were sealed so there would
be no public information. It was felt that a child did not need

a lawyer, for everyone concerned claimed to have in mind only "what is in the child's best interest." But not everyone agreed about that.

Changes and Reforms
in Juvenile Justice

In 1967, the Gault decision was handed down from the U.S. Supreme Court. It claimed that the private and informal procedures used by juvenile courts deprived children of certain rights of counsel (an attorney). It ruled that a juvenile who is accused of breaking the law must be granted the following rights:

- The right of counsel, and the parents to be given adequate notice of the specific charges (the accusation)

- To have counsel present during any case that might result in confinement (being sent to some controlled setting)

- To question witnesses

- To remain silent

- To have a prompt detention hearing

- To have a review hearing on an annual basis in all dependency and neglect cases.

Over the years, various rights for children have been gained through:

- Decisions of the Supreme Court

- Laws passed by states

- Laws passed by Congress

- Decisions by federal, state, and local courts.

The Supreme Court has used the Ninth Amendment and the Fourteenth Amendment to protect children.

> The Ninth Amendment guarantees that rights not listed in the Constitution are still held by the people.

By saying *the people*, they meant all people regardless of age. The founding fathers added this amendment because they knew that they could not list all of the rights of citizens. They didn't want to exclude any group of people in any circumstance.

In some cases the Supreme Court has ruled that children are also protected by the Fourteenth Amendment, which says in part:

> ". . . . nor shall any state deprive any person of life, liberty, or property without due process of law."

Types of Juvenile Cases

It is important to remember that not all juveniles who come before the courts are accused of breaking the law. As early as 1915, the legislature made a distinction between *dependent and neglected* children and *delinquent* children. If a child had no family that could or would care for him, he was considered a dependent child and was probably made a *ward of the court*. Unfortunately, these children often were sent to large institutions and treated like prisoners. Many times they were placed in settings with tough, angry delinquents, and the dependent children learned bad habits and suffered cruel handling. Read further to learn how dependent children are treated nowadays.

Today there are three distinct types of juvenile cases: dependency, status offense, and delinquency.

Dependency Cases

Dependency cases involve children who are victims of neglect or are abused children. Such situations would include children who live with one or more parent who is physically dangerous to the public or who might have a mental or physical deficiency, children who live with anyone whose behavior makes them unable to care for them properly. The emphasis is not on the child's behavior, but on the behavior of the parent or guardian. When a petition of neglect or abuse is made, the juvenile justice system will do what is necessary to protect the child. The child might be placed immediately in a temporary foster home. If the neglect or abuse is confirmed after careful investigations and hearings, the parent may be required to get counseling and could be punished. The child might even be taken away from the parent and placed in a foster or adoptive home.

Status Offense Cases

Status offense cases involve actions by minors which are not criminal, but are brought to the attention of the juvenile authority. Such behavior might be running away from home, habitual truancy from school, violation of a curfew, or violation of other ordinances (local laws) based on age. These are *status offenses*, not crimes. If an adult did these things, it would not be illegal. In some cases, juveniles are taken into custody because they can't control themselves and need help. Perhaps they caused trouble for their parents, or school, or community. Perhaps they left home and were considered "out of control" (of their family). Parents can even ask the court to have a child removed from the home. When this is done, it is usually because the juvenile is a danger to himself or to others in the home.

Status offenses can lead to a court declaration that the child is a "person in need of supervision." He or she can be placed at home or with a foster family or state juvenile camp or other facility (separate from delinquents). Wherever he is placed, the court maintains an interest and authority over the child. In a few states, status offenders are classified as juvenile delinquents, especially if they get into trouble again. If that happens, they can be sent to a training school or other more secure facility.

State laws differ on the treatment of status offenders, but in a general way the court procedures are the same as for delinquency cases.

Delinquency Cases

Delinquency cases involve actions which are illegal for a minor or juvenile. There are many offenses that are against the law for a juvenile, but not illegal for adults. Drinking alcohol is illegal if you are under the age of twenty-one years. Specific offenses commonly charged against juveniles include:

- Property crimes such as burglary, theft, and vandalism

- Crimes such as assault

- Public intoxication

- Use of illegal substances, that is, drugs

- Disorderly conduct

- "Joy-riding" (driving someone's car without that person's permission)

- Driving without a license

- Status offenses

In juvenile justice, proved offenders are usually convicted for *delinquency* rather than for the specific offense. This does not include very serious crimes such as murder.

How Juvenile Offenses Are Treated

Detention
Police may hold juveniles who are accused of violating the law. The police may also hold a juvenile in protective custody, either for being involved in questionable circumstances or for being with a person who was arrested. The juvenile's detention is not called *arrest*. It is being *taken into custody*.

Juveniles are handled differently than adult suspects. Depending on the specific circumstances, juveniles will either be released directly to their parents or be taken to the police department for short-term detention and processing. There are very specific rules for the treatment of juveniles when being held by police or the sheriff.

Release to Parents or Guardians
In most cases juveniles can be released to their parents or legal guardians within two hours of the arrest. However, serious cases requiring more investigation may require longer detention of the suspect, who might be held in a secure setting such as Juvenile Hall. Juveniles who are thought to be a danger to others or themselves can also be placed in Juvenile Hall. In all cases, however, an officer will notify parents or guardians that their child is in custody. The officer will also tell them the reasons why the action is being taken.

Juvenile Court Hearings
Where evidence supports charges against a juvenile suspect, and where the child is kept in custody, the case is referred to

the juvenile probation department or other officials, depending on the state. Each case is screened before a decision is made to seek court action or to use other corrective measures.

After attorneys, probation officers, arresting officers, and welfare workers have a chance to gather all the information they think necessary, a hearing before a judge is held to introduce all the evidence. Everyone involved with the child has a chance to speak in court. These hearings are more informal than the procedures in adult court. There is almost never a jury. In most states they are closed hearings, not open to the public or the press.

If the judge decides that the juvenile is delinquent or in need of supervision, he or she first declares the juvenile to be a *ward of the court*. This means the court will have a continuing interest and authority over the youngster. The judge then decides whether to send the juvenile to a group home, a camp for juveniles, Juvenile Hall, or any other setting provided for this purpose. For some cases, a separate *dispositional hearing* will be held to make the decision. Status offenders are not placed with delinquents except in special circumstances such as repeated offenses.

Juvenile courts try to balance justice with help and guidance for young people in trouble. In a legal way they act as a parent protecting a child. Most offenders younger than ten years old are not held legally accountable for their actions, and are not sent anywhere just for purposes of punishment. Rather, they may be turned over to child protective services or to some sheltered setting. If a young child is sent to Juvenile Hall, he will be separated from older juveniles who are accused or have been convicted of breaking the law. Even in placing older juveniles, the court aims for rehabilitation rather than punishment. The judge may decide on a training school, camp, Juvenile Hall, or other place that meets the youngster's needs.

Probation

Of course, the court may release the juvenile on probation, either right away or after some time in a facility. Probation allows the juvenile to return home while still under control of the court. He or she must regularly report to a probation officer and must comply with all "conditions of probation." If probation is violated, the youngster can go right back into custody. Here's a typical set of these probation conditions. The juvenile must:

- Inform parents of whereabouts at all times

- Not stay away from home without permission

- Be in legal residence between ten P.M. and six A.M. (this is like a curfew)

- Make restitution to the victim (for example, if a bike was stolen, the juvenile must return it or pay for it)

- Attend school

- Obey school rules (if not, it is a violation of probation)

- Participate in an approved program at school if not in the regular program

- Have absolutely no contact with persons not approved by parents or the parole officer

- Have no gang participation

- Have no contact with anyone involved in drugs or alcohol

- Attend a counseling program

- Spend a specified number of weekends at a juvenile work project

- Submit to search and seizure at any time requested

- Forfeit his or her driver's license, which is suspended for one year

And the juvenile will remain a ward of the court for some months or years.

As you can see, juveniles who have broken the law or who are legally considered "persons in need of supervision" are treated fairly but firmly. Just because they are children or minors does not prevent some of them from causing great danger and harm to others.

Some Very Serious Developments

Earlier in this chapter, I said that children have rights, but they also have responsibilities. More and more children are demanding adult privileges, and more and more children are committing serious crimes, adult crimes. Society hears of gang killings, children running around with guns and knives, children using drugs and stealing property to get money for drugs, children shoplifting just for the thrill, children drinking and driving, or children racing cars recklessly. Our juvenile justice system was designed for dealing with youth very different from the juveniles of today. Society is beginning to express strong feelings—many people want to have those children treated like adults and punished as adults.

When a boy is six feet tall, weighs 150 pounds, and beats up a smaller man, it is hard to think of that boy as a poor little child. When a juvenile has a gun, he or she can end someone's life. When a gang gets together to create a force, that gang has more power than any individual they might decide to pick on. We have all seen rioting on television, and it is frightening to see force without restraint.

Our society is not prepared to deal with the level of violence we see now. Early juvenile justice focused on the protection of the juvenile who "got into trouble." It was based on changing the child's behavior—to put the child in an environment that would help him or her to learn acceptable reactions and responses. Our focus now is to put the "kid" away to protect society. The present Attorney-General, Janet Reno, has said this often.

It is estimated that two-thirds of all crimes of burglary, arson, and robbery are committed by juveniles. One in every five juvenile crimes is committed by a young woman.

These are pretty heavy things to think about, but they are happening in your world. They happen in your school. They happen on the streets that you must share. They happen now more than ever before.

As new laws evolve, as new ways of dealing with children are designed, you will be asked to make important decisions. Some of you will be peace officers. Some of you may be attorneys, judges, or lawmakers. Many of you will be parents. Sad to say, some of you will be victims. But ALL of you will have the power of the vote. Use it well to protect yourself.

Chapter 15
CHALLENGES

Our justice system is constantly being challenged, sometimes by noisy, angry groups. This is not pleasant, but it is very exciting. All American people live within this system and must obey the laws. The taxpayer pays for this system and the voters create or change it, so it is very important that all our people participate in the system. If they do not like it, they can challenge it. A good system will not be destroyed by a challenge.

Some challenges are good and create good changes. This was certainly true when challenge resulted in the vote for black people and for women. If a challenge is not good, we hope it will not gather support and it will fail. Each challenge is serious, especially to the group making it. We must watch and be informed and participate. Don't sit back and just let everyone else care.

The First Amendment to our Constitution grants our freedom to assemble and protest and challenge and make feelings known. That is such a precious right that it is worth the discomfort of having people shouting and yelling and challenging. Of course, the only way we should challenge anything is to do it legally.

Recently a rock star produced an album with a song about the police and how terrible he thought they were.

The singer kept saying he wanted to kill the police. He called them names and said over and over that everyone should kill them. This really bothered me and it bothered many other people. Most wanted the album taken out of the stores. The people who produced the album claimed their First Amendment rights to free speech. The producers were within their constitutional rights. The exciting part of this story was that "the people" didn't attack the First Amendment and demand that the government do something about this situation. Sure, some wanted the police to move in and take the albums out of stores and burn them—but that is so dangerous. There might come a time when some group could demand other things be burned, things we care about and really believe in.

The people who objected to the record used their own power. They wrote to the manufacturer and voiced their objections. They talked to TV and newspaper reporters. They threatened to boycott the record company (refuse to buy their products). They also threatened to boycott the distributors and the companies that supply the materials to make the records. They condemned the singer openly in the news—which was well within their own First Amendment rights.

The record company backed down. They removed the albums from the stores. They were worried about future sales and having customers angry with them.

This is a terrific example of people taking charge of their lives, meeting challenges, and using their constitutional rights for changes without abusing the law. We don't have to put up with things we feel are disgusting, dangerous, or wrong. Get involved!

By challenges, we are forced to look again and examine over and over what we are doing. These challenges also make our Constitution so very precious. Remember this as you read about the Constitution now.

Chapter 16
THE CONSTITUTION OF THE UNITED STATES

The United States Constitution is the supreme law of the land. It establishes the form of the United States government and defines the rights and liberties of the American people. It fulfills the statement in the Declaration of Independence:

> "We hold these truths to be self-evident—that all men are created equal; that they are endowed by their Creator with certain unalienable rights; that among these are life, liberty and the pursuit of happiness."

This famous Declaration of Independence was issued by the American colonies when they got together to declare themselves free from England before the Revolutionary War. Do realize that this declaration stated that people are endowed with the right to the *pursuit* of happiness. It did not say that all have the *right* to happiness. It did not say that the government must make you happy. It did not say that you have the right to be happy at anyone's expense. It meant that you have the right to earn, or find, or create (to pursue) happiness for yourself. No one owes happiness to you. Your rights must be shared with all people who also have those same rights.

How the National Government Began

After the Declaration of Independence, it was necessary to form a strong nation under which each person could live peacefully and free. The colonies had their own small governments. They issued their own money, had their own taxes, their own laws, and so on. It soon became obvious that there were many concerns that affected all the colonies. It was necessary to form a central government. This didn't mean that the colonists would lose all their power. It meant that under a united government, these colonies or states could take part in the affairs of the whole country. There could be one currency, one army, laws governing all people, fair taxes, and so forth.

There were many problems in America after the Revolutionary War. There was a tremendous debt to pay, because war is very expensive. In some areas men were settling their problems by taking up arms (that means using weapons—guns). There was no definite law enforcement against it where they lived. Some states charged huge taxes to other states if they wanted to trade goods. Some states passed laws that were unjust.

In an effort to solve these problems, the new states joined together in a confederation, which was a group of loosely united, independent states. They wrote a document to define this system, called the Articles of Confederation, which was adopted in 1777. It was a good attempt, but the states didn't work together well enough. Leaders from each state felt it was time to end these troubles. The only way to get peace and order was to form a new, stronger, central government.

The Constitutional Convention

Representatives from five states met and agreed to summon the states to a convention to work on revising the Articles of Confederation. Seventy-four delegates from twelve states were appointed to meet for a Constitutional Convention. Only Rhode Island refused to send a delegation. Other states responded, and on May 14, 1787, fifty-five delegates attended. Thirty-nine delegates stayed to the end and signed this powerful document. The delegates did far more than they were asked. Instead of merely revising the Articles of Confederation, they wrote a remarkable plan of government: the Constitution of the United States of America—in Convention, September 17, 1787.

The Constitution

The Constitution starts with a short statement telling the purpose or goals of this new government. It is called the Preamble, and it very simply establishes the purpose and authority of the national government.

> We the people of the United States, in order to form a more perfect union, establish justice, insure domestic tranquillity, provide for the common defense, promote the general welfare, and secure the blessings of liberty to ourselves and our posterity, do ordain and establish this Constitution for the United States of America.

With these goals in mind, the Constitution established a strong national government, divided into three equal branches: the legislative branch, the executive branch, and the judicial branch.

The legislative branch was established first. The writers of the Constitution wanted to make sure they were not putting all the power in one leader, such as the president. They wanted to divide the power among the people, so they gave all law-making power to Congress, that is, to the legislature. Congress is the legislative branch of our government. It consists of the House of Representatives, and the Senate.

The executive branch was set up with an elected president as the head of the government. The executive branch, led by the president, enforces the laws.

The judicial branch was formed with its power in the Supreme Court, a group of judges appointed by the president and approved by the Senate. The Supreme Court was and is the final judge of what the Constitution means. Its main purpose is to judge whether any law or legal action agrees with the Constitution. This is called *judging the constitutionality* of decisions. The Supreme Court also has power in such things as treaties, controversies between states, cases involving ambassadors or foreign ministers, and maritime law.

The Constitution that the delegates wrote in 1787 was only a few pages long. It consisted of just seven "articles."

- Articles One, Two, and Three dealt with the legislature (lawmakers), the judiciary (the Supreme Court), and the executive (the president and vice-president).

- Article Four covered the relations between the states.

- Article Five provided for amending (changing) the Constitution in the future.

- Article Six dealt with many different details that were not covered in the first five articles, like debts owed by the Confederation, foreign treaties, and qualifications for office.

- Article Seven explained how the Constitution would be *ratified*, that is, how the states would accept it and vote it into being.

These seven articles set forth the organization of the new government. They didn't have a lot of words nor did they spell out every fine detail of government. The Constitution was flexible. The delegates knew that things change from time to time, and they wanted this constitution to last a long time. They wanted it to be responsive to change.

The Bill of Rights

As the Constitution was being voted on by the delegates, the Constitutional Convention recommended that a Bill of Rights be appended (added). To do this, they wrote the first ten amendments to the Constitution, which set forth a list of rights for citizens and limits on government power. The object of the Bill of Rights was to stop government from creating the abuses of power that the English colonies had known under King George III. The next chapter of this book tells about the Bill of Rights and the later amendments to the Constitution.

Getting a Better Understanding

You are young people, and I am talking about things that happened a long time ago. These are things that really do not concern you now, things that you cannot change or do anything about right now. Your world is concerned with growing and learning; it is the world of young people—the world of today.

As we think about those men who tried to form a new nation a long time ago, and as we read what they designed, maybe you can feel some of the excitement they must have felt about this country's future. Perhaps, instead of just reading about it, it would be helpful if you did the same thing those early leaders did, right now. In the Activities and Games at the end of this book, there is a section called "Freedomland." This explains how you and some friends can act out designing a new government, and some of the things you have to think about, step by step. If you could do this activity before going on to read the next chapter, it would help you appreciate the wisdom of the men who wrote the Constitution and the Bill of Rights.

Chapter 17
AMENDMENTS TO
THE CONSTITUTION

This book has mentioned *amendments* (changes) to the Constitution many times, amendments that have a direct effect on your rights as a citizen. We have discussed the various rights guaranteed by these amendments. Let's consider them in more detail, one by one. (You are about to read some of the longest sentences you have ever seen. Just stick with it—it is hard to stay connected, but you can do it.)

As we saw in the last chapter, the first ten amendments were written quite soon after the Constitution. They are called *The Bill of Rights* and they spell out our basic rights.

The First Amendment (1791)

Section 1: "Congress shall make no law respecting an establishment of religion, or prohibiting the free exercise thereof; or abridging the freedom of speech, or of the press; or the right of the people peaceably to assemble, and to petition the government for a redress of grievances."

This amendment gave people the freedom to worship in whatever way they wanted. It allowed people to speak out about any issue and to say what they wanted as long as it didn't hurt anyone. The government could not punish someone for speaking out unless what they said created a "clear and present danger."

We hear this called the *free speech amendment*. By freedom of the press, newspapers were free to print whatever they wanted as long as they didn't deliberately set out to lie or hurt anyone. When information threatened the national security, a problem arose; and there was, and still is, active debate about any limiting of the freedom of the press.

Freedom of assembly meant that people could gather peaceably for any legal purpose. It gave people the freedom to tell the government what they thought was wrong and to ask for a change or help. Even when groups wanted to discuss changing the government, their right to gather together and speak freely was and is guaranteed by the Constitution. It is this very right that makes our government so precious, and we must defend this and other rights always. We must also act in a way that does not abuse these freedoms.

The Second Amendment (1791)

> Section 1: "A well-regulated militia being necessary to the security of a free state, the right of the people to keep and bear arms shall not be infringed."

Many people think this amendment gives people the right to carry guns, and it is quoted often now that gun control is a big issue. But we should remember that it was written at a time when the country did not have police forces and a national guard.

A militia was an army of citizens organized to defend the people in an emergency. It is different from an army made up of professional soldiers. In the early days, when the United States did not keep a peacetime army or a national guard, militias were used when necessary.

This amendment uses the term *being necessary*, which means "if it becomes necessary," and then adds that the rights of people to bear arms shall not be infringed (taken away or disturbed). There are people who use this to demand their right to own and use a gun at any time. There are others who interpret the amendment as saying that we have this right only when an emergency exists, as in time of war or invasion.

The Third Amendment (1791)

Section 1: "No soldier shall, in time of peace, be quartered in any house without the consent of the owner, nor in time of war, but in a manner to be prescribed by law."

This amendment gave people the right to be secure in their own homes. Because of the Third Amendment, a soldier cannot knock on someone's door and demand to be taken in or to live there. This amendment makes sure the government cannot take over your home or business and house their army. The quartering of soldiers was a problem in those early days, but we do not have this problem today.

The Fourth Amendment (1791)

Section 1: "The right of the people to be secure in their persons, houses, papers, and effects, against unreasonable searches and seizures, shall not be violated, and no warrants shall be issued but upon probable cause, supported by oath or affirmation, and particularly describing the place to be searched, and the persons or things to be seized."

This amendment assured the people that the police could not invade their homes and take anything without legal permission, which is called a *warrant*. This permission is issued after the person seeking it swears to a judge that he has probable cause for the search. (*Probable cause* means a good reason, and he must tell the judge what that reason is.) The warrant is issued by a judge. The seizure part of the amendment meant that a person could not be arrested except by a warrant sworn for that purpose.

A new concern is about the fact that persons with computers can enter the computer files of a business and read private papers or plans without even entering the office of the business. This is an invasion of privacy. If the police or some private group put a recording device in your office or put a "tap" on your telephone; if they monitor the files on your computer, is any of this in violation of the rights guaranteed in this amendment?

The Fifth Amendment (1791)

Section 1: "No person shall be held to answer for a capital, or otherwise infamous crime, unless on a presentment or indictment of a grand jury, except in cases arising in the land or naval forces, or in the militia when in actual service in time of war or public danger; nor shall any person be subject for the same offense to be twice put in jeopardy of life or limb; nor shall be compelled in any criminal case to be a witness against himself, nor be deprived of life, liberty, or property, without due process of law; nor shall private property be taken for public use without just compensation."

This amendment outlines the rights of a person when indicted (formally accused) of a capital crime or other serious crime. (A *capital crime* is one that can be punished by death.)

The Fifth Amendment insures that a person cannot be called as a witness against himself in any criminal trial. This is why the prosecution cannot call a defendant to testify at his own trial. However, the prosecution can cross-examine if the defendant is called to the witness stand by his own lawyer. The spouse of a defendant cannot be required to testify against him or her. When you hear of someone pleading "Fifth Amendment rights," this is what is meant. If a witness has been asked for testimony that might tend to *incriminate* him (cause him to be accused of a crime), the Fifth Amendment gives him the right not to answer.

It is important to realize that our government cannot grab a person, imprison and question him so they can hear something they can use to find him guilty of a deed. This amendment guarantees a "due process of law." That means that a person held for a crime is entitled to a trial and the protection of all of his rights that the Constitution guarantees him throughout the process of the trial. These rights are explained in more detail in the Fourteenth Amendment.

The Fifth Amendment also guarantees that a person does not have to stand trial for the same charge more than once. If he was found not guilty the first time, he does not have to go through the agony of a second trial. The federal authorities had to bring new charges against the police in order to stage a second trial in the Rodney King beating case.

Isn't it amazing that all the rights mentioned—and more— are covered by those few words in this amendment? The framers of the Constitution worked hard to choose just the right words so that even two hundred years later we can still use their ideas and apply them to the way we live now.

The Sixth Amendment (1791)

Section 1: "In all criminal prosecutions, the accused shall enjoy the right to a speedy and public trial, by an impartial jury of the state and district wherein the crime shall have been committed, which district shall have been previously ascertained by law, and to be informed of the nature and cause of the accusation; to be confronted with the witnesses against him; to have compulsory process for obtaining witnesses in his favor; and to have the assistance of counsel for his defense."

This amendment establishes the protection guaranteed a person being arrested or accused of a crime. As explained in this book's chapters on arrest and trial, these protective rights are observed in the arrest, booking, and trial procedures we now use.

Most of these guarantees are stated in the Miranda Warning, which is quoted on page 63 in Chapter 11. An accused person has the right to a speedy and public trial by a fair jury of the state and community where the crime was committed. If there is a very good reason for holding the trial somewhere else, the attorneys may ask for a *change of venue*. If the court agrees, another city or town is chosen.

The arrested person has the right to be told the nature of the crime for which he was arrested. He has the power to subpoena witnesses (legally require them to appear in court) and to gather evidence. And he has the right to have an attorney to aid in his defense. If the accused cannot afford an attorney, one will be provided for him.

I want to emphasize again that our system of justice accuses the person and then has to prove it. That person is considered innocent until proved guilty. The accused person has powerful protections of his or her rights under the Constitution, particularly under the Fifth, Sixth, Eighth, Ninth, Tenth, and Fourteenth Amendments.

The Seventh Amendment (1791)

> Section 1: "In suits at common law, where the value in controversy shall exceed twenty dollars, the right of trial by jury shall be preserved, and no fact tried by a jury, shall be otherwise reexamined in any other court of the United States, than according to the rules of common law."

This amendment refers to civil law, which is concerned with disputes (fights or disagreements) among people, businesses, or institutions. Disputes that are dealt with under civil law are not crimes. When people disagree and want a legal solution which both sides must uphold, they may start a civil suit and bring that disagreement to court.

A trial by jury is a most important guarantee. By allowing a jury of peers (ordinary people like you and me), we hope for the fairest decision. The sum of twenty dollars mentioned in this amendment is still valid in federal law if someone demanded this right. It is almost never challenged. In the days when the amendment was written, twenty dollars was a great deal of money.

The Eighth Amendment (1791)

"Excessive bail shall not be required, nor excessive fines imposed, nor cruel and unusual punishments inflicted."

This amendment is examined over and over. Because of it, the standards for jails and prisons are inspected to see if prisoners are suffering from unusually bad conditions. A judge or jury cannot decide to punish someone in a way that most people would consider cruel or unusual. For instance, physical torture is not allowed, and any punishment should not be too severe for the crime. A person could not be sent to jail for many years because of a minor offense committed for the first time.

The greatest challenge to the Eighth Amendment is over the death penalty. Many people feel that execution is cruel and unusual punishment. In many states, before a person is executed his or her "case" is reviewed over and over, going from one court of appeal to another, and finally must be reviewed by the Supreme Court of the state where the trial was held. The appeal and review process can take many years and is very expensive, but many judges feel that they would rather see ninety-nine guilty persons go free than to see one innocent person punished unjustly.

The provisions against excessive bail and fines mean that justice is available to poor people as well as people with a lot of money.

Because of the guarantees in the Eighth Amendment, we constantly question if we are doing right by people who have been accused and/or convicted of crimes, or if things need to be reexamined and done differently.

The Ninth Amendment (1791)

Section 1: "The enumeration in the Constitution of certain rights shall not be construed to deny or disparage others retained by the people."

This statement means that the people have more rights than those guaranteed in the Constitution. The framers of the Constitution did not want to list every right, for to do so would take hundreds of pages, and then they would still leave some out.

Instead, they wrote an amendment that allows us to interpret what they meant. Some people claim it means we have a right to privacy. The Ninth Amendment is used by many people now to say that whatever they want to do within their own home or other space is constitutional and therefore legal. It is an amendment that is not very specific about what it guarantees—and that is on purpose.

Many Supreme Court justices have written opinions of the meaning of this amendment. Few of them agree on an exact definition. The opinions will continue as this amendment is reexamined in the future. Perhaps one of you will some day serve on the Supreme Court and add to the definitions of these rights.

The Tenth Amendment (1791)

Section 1: "The powers not delegated to the United States by the Constitution nor prohibited by it to the states, are reserved to the states respectively or to the people."

The Tenth Amendment was an attempt to keep a balance between the rights of the government of the United States and the rights of the governments of the individual states. The result is that different states have different laws and rulings about such things as using the death penalty, marriage, inheritance, welfare, crime, and the use of alcohol and drugs.

States have their own courts, their own laws, their own justice systems, which involve only the people of that state. After the American Revolution, the states inherited a sovereign's role, which means they were supreme and independent. Then as our central (federal) government was being formed, these states gave some powers to the new United States government. The federal government has authority over only a part of our lives. States and towns have other powers. And we individuals have some rights that no laws can touch, except in special circumstances. (In time of war, many rules or laws can be enacted that cannot be imposed in peacetime.)

Of course a state may not pass a law that is unconstitutional. One state cannot pass a law that would be unfair to the people of another state. If it did, the issue would be solved in a federal court. Even though each state has its own constitution, the states must rule within the principles of the Constitution of the United States.

More Amendments Followed the Bill of Rights

These first ten amendments, called the Bill of Rights, were all written in 1791. They made standard throughout the United States the just and basic rights the new federal government guaranteed to every citizen. The rest of the amendments to the Constitution follow the history of our country as America went through wars, recognized important rights not covered in the earlier amendments, and grew to be the huge nation it is today. It reads like a time line.

The Eleventh Amendment (1795)

Section 1: "The judicial power of the United States shall not be construed to extend to any suit or law or equity, commenced or prosecuted against one of the United States by citizens of another state, or by citizens or subjects of any foreign states."

This amendment states that if a citizen of one state sues a citizen of another state, the suit may not be tried in a federal court. The suit must be tried in the state courts. The same is true if a person from another country sues a citizen of a state.

The Twelfth Amendment (1804)

Take a big breath for this amendment. It is really long and difficult to read.

Section 1: "The electors shall meet in their respective states and vote by ballot for president and vice-president, one of whom, at least, shall not be an inhabitant of the same state with themselves; they shall name in their ballots the person voted for as president, and in distinct ballots the person voted for as vice-president; and they shall make distinct lists of all persons voted for as president, and of all persons voted for as vice-president, and of the number of votes for each, which lists they shall sign and certify, and transmit sealed to the seat of the government of the United States, directed to the president of the Senate;—the president of the Senate shall, in the presence of the Senate and the House of Representatives, open all the certificates and the votes shall then be counted;—the person having the greatest number of votes for president, shall be the president, if such number be a majority of the whole number of electors appointed; and if no person have such majority, then from the persons having the highest numbers not exceeding three on the list of those voted for as president, the House of Representatives shall choose immediately, by ballot, the president.

"But in choosing the president, the votes shall be taken by states, the representation from each state having one vote; a quorum for this purpose shall consist of a member or members from two-thirds of the states, and a majority of all the states shall be necessary to a choice.

"And if the House of Representatives shall not choose a president whenever the right of choice shall devolve upon them before the fourth day of March next following, then the vice-president shall act as president, as in the case of the death or other constitutional disability of the president.—The person having the greatest number of votes as vice-president shall be the vice-president, if such number be a majority of the whole number of electors appointed, and if no person have a majority, then from the two highest numbers on the list, the Senate shall choose the vice-president; a quorum for that purpose shall consist of two-thirds of the whole number of senators, and a majority of the whole number shall be necessary to a choice. But no person constitutionally ineligible to the office of president shall be eligible to that of vice-president of the United States."

Whew! That's a lot of words—in fact the first sentence has 206 words—and that makes it very hard for us to understand. But the people working on our laws in 1804 wanted it to be very clear how the counting of votes was to take place, and how the choosing of the president and vice-president was to be done.

When so many words are used to express an idea, we have to take the sentences apart, analyze each part and have them relate to the whole thought. Using many words is the way a lot of laws, contracts, and other legal papers are written—to make each meaning specific and try to make it impossible to misunderstand. After you have studied law, this legal language becomes easier to read, but never really easy. (Some people call it *legalese*.)

One thing to notice about the Twelfth Amendment is that *electors* actually choose the president and vice-president (unless they can't reach a majority, in which case the Congress must choose). Here's the way it works. In the primary elections, citizens vote to decide who will be put on the ballot. Then comes the general election, when the citizens' votes are counted to choose electors. This is called the popular vote. In each state the electors are instructed and sent to the *electoral college* (college means "meeting" in this case), to select the president and vice-president following the lead of the popular vote.

Notice also that the amendment made it very clear that the vice-president is elected separately. He or she is not a "runner-up" in the vote for president.

The Thirteenth Amendment (1865)

> Section 1: "Neither slavery or involuntary servitude, except as a punishment for crime whereof the party shall have been duly convicted, shall exist within the United States, or any place subject to their jurisdiction."
>
> Section 2: "Congress shall have the power to enforce this article by appropriate legislation."

This "Section 2" started a trend that followed in the remaining amendments. In each one, the government is granted the "power to enforce." Although the Supreme Court rules on the constitutionality of an amendment, the power to enforce the amendment is given to the legislature—our Congress.

It is very clear that this amendment guarantees that no person can be treated as a slave. It prohibits involuntary servitude (people being held or used as slaves or people being forced to work if they don't want to, or to work without being paid). This means that one person can never "own" another.

The Fourteenth Amendment (1868)

Section 1: "All persons born or naturalized in the United States, and subject to the jurisdiction thereof, are citizens of the United States and of the state wherein they reside. No state shall make or enforce any law which shall abridge the privileges or immunities of citizens of the United States; nor shall any state deprive any person of life, liberty, or property, without due process of law; nor deny to any person within its jurisdiction the equal protection of the laws."

Section 2: "Representatives shall be apportioned among the several states according to their respective numbers, counting the whole number of persons in each state, excluding Indians not taxed.

"But when the right to vote at any election for the choice of electors for president and vice-president of the United States, representatives in Congress, the executive and judicial officers of a state, or the members of the legislature thereof is denied to any of the male members of such state being of twenty-one years of age, and citizens of the United States, or in any way abridged, except for participation in rebellion, or other crime, the basis of representation therein shall be reduced in the proportion which the number of such male citizens shall bear to the whole number of male citizens twenty-one years of age in such state."

Section 3: "No person shall be a senator or representative in Congress, or elector of president and vice-president, or hold any office, civil or military, under the United States, or under any state, who having previously taken an oath, as a member of Congress, or as an officer of the United States, or as a member of any state legislature, or as an executive or judicial officer of any state, to support the Constitution of the United States, shall have engaged in insurrection or rebellion against the same, or given aid or comfort to the enemies thereof. But Congress may by a vote of two-thirds of each house, remove such disability."

This amendment was written to protect the rights of the freed slaves and all other men. (Note that the amendment speaks only of men. The right to vote was not extended to women at this time.) Along with the Bill of Rights the Fourteenth Amendment protects rights of citizens in regards to citizenship and representation. It states that all persons born here or naturalized (persons who moved to our country, passed the necessary tests for citizenship and have sworn an oath of allegiance) are considered citizens of the United States, and male citizens who are twenty-one years of age or older may vote.

Section 2 of the amendment provided that if any male citizen over twenty-one is not allowed to vote, he cannot be included in the count that determines how many representatives the state is allowed in the Congress. Section 3 said that no person could hold a federal office if he has engaged in any rebellion against the United States, or given aid or comfort to any enemies of the government. This includes those who participated in the Civil War.

Section 4: "The validity of the public debt of the United States, authorized by law, including debts incurred for payment of pensions and bounties for services in suppressing insurrection or rebellion, shall not be questioned. But neither the United States nor any state shall assume or pay any debt or obligation incurred in aid of insurrection or rebellion against the United States, or any claim for the loss or emancipation of any slave; but all such debts, obligations and claims shall be held illegal and void."

Section 5: "The Congress shall have power to enforce, by appropriate legislation, the provisions of this article."

Section 4, obviously, dealt with special problems that could have arisen after the Civil War.

The Fifteenth Amendment
(1870)

Section 1: "The right of citizens of the United States to vote shall not be denied or abridged by the United States or by any state on account of race, color, or previous condition of servitude."

   Section 2: "The Congress shall have power to enforce this article by appropriate legislation."

This amendment protects the voting rights of all male citizens. It made it very clear that the right to vote was assured to male black citizens.

The Sixteenth Amendment
(1913)

Section 1: "The Congress shall have power to lay and collect taxes on incomes, from whatever source derived, without apportionment among the several states, and without regard to any census or enumeration."

This amendment gave Congress the power to establish an income tax, which we still have today.

The Seventeenth Amendment
(1913)

Section 1: "The Senate of the United States shall be composed of two senators from each state, elected by the people thereof, for six years; and each senator shall have one vote. The electors in each state shall have the qualifications requisite for electors of the most numerous branch of the state legislatures.

"When vacancies happen in the representation of any state in the Senate, the executive authority of such state shall issue writs of elections to fill such vacancies: provided that the legislature of any state may empower the executive thereof to make temporary appointments until the people fill the vacancies by election as the legislature may direct.

"This amendment shall not be so construed to affect the election or term of any senator chosen before it becomes valid as part of the Constitution."

This amendment provided that the "people" would elect their own U.S. senators and it outlined the process for electing them.

The Eighteenth Amendment (1919)

Section 1: "After one year after the ratification of this article, the manufacture, sale, or transportation of intoxicating liquors within the United States and all territory subject to the jurisdiction thereof for beverage purposes is hereby prohibited."

Section 2: "The Congress and the several states shall have concurrent power to enforce this article by appropriate legislation."

Section 3: "This article shall be inoperative unless it shall have been ratified as an amendment to the Constitution by the legislatures of the several states, as provided in the Constitution, within seven years from the date of the submission hereof to the states by the Congress."

The Eighteenth Amendment made it illegal to manufacture, sell, or transport intoxicating liquors (alcohol) within the United States, or to import or export liquor for beverage purposes. The process was called *Prohibition*.

The Nineteenth Amendment
(1920)

Section 1: "The right of citizens of the United States to vote shall not be denied or abridged by the United States or by any state on account of sex."

Section 2: "Congress shall have the power to enforce this article by appropriate legislation."

This amendment granted to all citizens the right to vote regardless of sex. In other words, it allowed women to vote. At that time this meant that 26 million voters were added to the U.S. government election process. Remember, this amendment was passed by men who felt it was wrong that women were denied a share in forming and running our government.

The Twentieth Amendment
(1933)

Section 1: "The terms of the president and vice-president shall end at noon on the twentieth day of January, and the terms of senators and representatives at noon on the third day of January, of the years in which such terms would have ended if this article had not been ratified; and the terms of their successors shall then begin."

Section 2: "The Congress shall assemble at least once in every year, and such meeting shall begin at noon on the third day of January, unless they shall by law appoint a different day."

Section 3: "If at the time fixed for the beginning of the term of the president, the president elect shall have died, the vice-president elect shall become president. If a president shall not have been chosen before the time fixed for the beginning of his term, or if the president elect shall have failed to qualify, then the vice-president elect shall act as president until a president shall have qualified; and the Congress may by law provide for the case wherein neither a president elect nor a vice-president elect shall have qualified, declaring who shall then act as president, or the manner in which one who is to act shall be selected, and such person shall act accordingly until a president or vice-president shall have qualified."

Section 4: "The Congress may by law provide for the case of the death of any of the persons from whom the House of Representatives may choose a president whenever the right of choice shall have devolved upon them, and for the case of the death of any of the persons from whom the Senate may choose a vice-president whenever the right of choice shall have devolved upon them."

Section 5: "Sections 1 and 2 shall take effect on the fifteenth day of October following the ratification of this article."

Section 6: "This article shall be inoperative unless it shall have been ratified as an amendment to the Constitution by the legislatures of three-fourths of the several states within seven years from the date of its submission."

This amendment outlines the terms, and when these terms begin and end, for the president and vice-president. It also outlines when Congress shall assemble and how Congress proceeds if the president dies. It makes sure the government continues to function smoothly during the change of office and after elections.

The Twenty-first Amendment (1933)

Section 1: "The Eighteenth Article of Amendment to the Constitution of the United States is hereby repealed."

Section 2: "The transportation or importation into any state, territory, or possession of the United States for delivery or use therein of intoxicating liquors, in violation of the laws thereof, is hereby prohibited."

Section 3: "This article shall be inoperative unless it

> shall have been ratified as an amendment to the Constitution by conventions in the several states, as provided in the Constitution, within seven years from the date of the submission hereof to the states by Congress."

This is the first amendment that repealed (canceled) one of the earlier amendments. Do you remember that the Eighteenth Amendment made it illegal to make or sell alcoholic beverages (liquor)?

Section 2 seems to say that liquor is still prohibited, but that is not quite true. What it really says is that the government still has laws controlling the sale and use of alcoholic beverages, and people must obey them. It also means that individual states can make their own laws about liquor use, and those laws must be respected by other states.

It was important that the framers of the Constitution made it possible to add and take away amendments as the needs of the United States changed. What is really amazing is that the amendments were drawn up so well that in these two hundred years, only one amendment has been repealed or canceled. However, a few amendments have been updated, such as the age of voters in the Twenty-sixth Amendment.

The Twenty-second Amendment (1951)

> Section 1: "No person shall be elected to the office of the president more than twice, and no person who has held the office of president, or acted as president, for more than two years of a term to which some other person was elected president, shall be elected to the office of president more than once. But this article shall not apply to any person holding the office of president when this article was proposed by the Congress and shall not prevent any person who may be holding the office of president, or acting as president, during the term within which this article becomes operative from

holding the office of president or acting as president during the remainder of such term."

This amendment came after President Franklin D. Roosevelt was elected to a fourth term. Congress felt that it would be better if the president served only two terms and then a new candidate should come before the people. The rest of the amendment concerns the time a vice-president might serve if a president died or was taken out of office, especially if that person was elected as president after serving as acting president.

The Twenty-third Amendment (1961)

Section 1: "The district constituting the seat of government of the United States shall appoint in such manner as the Congress may direct:

"A number of electors of president and vice-president equal to the whole number of senators and representatives in Congress to which the district would be entitled if it were a state, but in no event more than the least populous state; they shall be in addition to those appointed by the states, but they shall be considered, for the purposes of the election of president and vice-president, to be electors appointed by a state; and they shall meet in the district and perform such duties as provided by the Twelfth Article of Amendment."

Section 2: "The Congress shall have power to enforce this article by appropriate legislation."

This amendment gives the people of Washington D.C. the right to vote. Remember that Washington D.C. is not a state, but it is a district called the District of Columbia, a special area that is set aside to be the "seat" of our government. This amendment tells how many electors they shall have and how that number is determined.

The Twenty-fourth Amendment (1964)

Section 1: "The right of citizens of the United States to vote in any primary or other election for president or vice-president, for electors for president or vice-president, or for senator or representative in Congress shall not be denied or abridged by the United States or any state by reason of failure to pay any poll tax or other tax."

Section 2: "Congress shall have power to enforce this article by appropriate legislation."

This amendment made it illegal to make people pay a tax (a poll tax) in order to vote. Voting is a *right* guaranteed to all citizens. There were people in some states who wanted to control who voted and who could not. They thought that if people had to pay a tax before voting, poor people might not be able to afford to vote. There were also places where people offered to pay your tax if you voted the way they told you. This was a terrible abuse of the right of all American citizens to vote.

The Twenty-fifth Amendment (1967)

Section 1: "In case of the removal of the president from office or of his death or resignation, the vice-president shall become president."

Section 2: "Whenever there is a vacancy in the office of the vice-president, the president shall nominate a vice-president who shall take office upon confirmation by a majority vote of both Houses of Congress."

Section 3: "Whenever the president transmits to the president pro tempore of the Senate and the speaker of the House of Representatives his written declaration that he is unable to discharge the powers and duties of his office, and until he transmits to them a written declaration to the contrary, such powers and duties shall be discharged by the vice-president as acting president."

Section 4: "Whenever the vice-president and a majority of either the principal officers of the executive departments or of such other body as Congress may by law provide, transmit to the president pro tempore of the Senate and the speaker of the House of Representatives their written declaration that the president is unable to discharge the powers and duties of his office, the vice-president shall immediately assume the powers and duties of the office as acting president.

"Thereafter, when the president transmits to the president pro tempore of the Senate and the speaker of the House of Representatives his written declaration that no inability exists, he shall resume the powers and duties of his office unless the vice-president and a majority of either the principal officers of the executive department or of such other body as Congress may by law provide, transmit within four days to the president pro tempore of the Senate and the speaker of the House of Representatives their written declaration that the president is unable to discharge the powers and duties of his office. Thereupon Congress shall decide the issue, assembling within forty-eight hours for that purpose if not in session. If the Congress, within twenty-one days after receipt of the latter written declaration, or if Congress is not in session, within twenty-one days after Congress is required to assemble, determines by two-thirds vote of both houses that the president is unable to discharge the powers and duties of this office, the vice-president shall continue to discharge the same as acting president; otherwise the president shall resume the powers and duties of his office."

Again we find words, and more words, but the legislature wants it perfectly clear how someone assumes the duties of president if the president becomes too ill or is in any other way unable to perform as president. There were to be no fights or power struggles. They established directions which would clearly insure that the transition of power be smooth and peaceful.

The Twenty-sixth Amendment (1971)

> Section 1: "The right of citizens of the United States, who are eighteen years of age or older, to vote shall not be denied or abridged by the United States or by any state on account of age."
>
> Section 2: "The Congress shall have power to enforce this article by appropriate legislation."

The voting age was lowered from twenty-one to eighteen years of age.

Constitutional Solutions for Problems

Some of the amendments that we just read do not affect us today. We do not have to worry about giving soldiers space in our homes (*quartering*). We don't think much about a poll tax. That is because people passed amendments and laws about these things at the time it was a problem. Most of today's problems are covered by the Constitution in a broad sense. In time to come there will probably be further amendments to the Constitution. Specific problems can be covered by laws that are based on the Constitution.

At the end of the previous chapter, I suggested that you try designing a constitution. Can you think of other things now that should have been in your constitution? Maybe it needs an amendment or two.

And can you think of things that are important now that were not a problem years ago when the U.S. Constitution and its amendments were written? Times certainly have changed. Scientific advancements have made our lives easier in many ways and more complicated in others. Think about it.

Chapter 18
IT'S ALL ABOUT YOU!

In the beginning I told you this is a book about law—and it is. But it is really a book about you, for you are the law, you are the government, you are the future, and you will be history.

Today you and I are living in the world our grandparents and great great grandparents made for us. Good or bad—this is what they left us. The wars we fight, the economy we must live with, the laws and form of government we must live under, were determined by them. We have to thank them for the schools and universities they established, the forests and parks that were grown, the medical and scientific inventions we enjoy, and the system of justice under which we live. But not everything is perfect, and often we are at a dangerous point of losing some hard-won benefits or freedoms.

I am older than you, so I should be able to change what I don't like. I can't change everything and make the whole country do things just the way I want. But I can get involved. I can speak and write and work and vote—and I do.

You are my future. You will be at your greatest power when I will be a very old lady. I need you. I want you to be active, to be just, to be smart, and to care. I want you to think about all the old people and I want you to think of all the new people—

the babies coming into the world, your children and your grandchildren.

Don't just sit back and say, "Oh, what can I do? I'm only one person. I'm just a kid."

A group called the Christophers have a saying: "It is better to light one candle than to curse the darkness." Try this sometime. Sit in a totally dark room and experience how impossible it seems to get anything done. Then light one little match. That burst of light is very dramatic. It makes such a difference. It gives you a chance to do something. Its time is short, but in that time you could grab a flashlight or locate the light switch or the telephone.

Now imagine if your whole class was with you and they each had one match. That means more power. It also means you will achieve the most if you work together. Together you can decide whether to light one match at a time so the light lasts longer, or to light them all at once to achieve a greater light. You might even decide to wait and only light a match at times of emergency.

The really interesting thing is that you may get to benefit from the other person's match. It may also be thought of as yours. This can make you care very much about what others do with their property. This is a little like the way we think about our planet now. What others do with their land and environment will affect us. If we realize that we will all share the "darkness," perhaps we will all share the thinking or responsibility for the best use of the resources we have.

You are so very important. In a few short years, we can say: "You have that one precious vote—you are the Constitution—you are the law—you are the government." And right now, you are the future. You are a citizen of the United States of America, and you are one of the luckiest, richest, most powerful people in the world.

ACTIVITIES AND GAMES

Creating a Law

This activity really needs enough friends or classmates to divide into the four groups mentioned. If you're on your own, you can still learn a lot by reading it carefully. Imagine that you are the bill! How many places you would go to and how many people you would meet!

I am going to tell you how a bill is introduced in Congress and what has to happen before it is made a law. This is a long process that goes on and on and on. To make it more meaningful for you and more fun, perhaps you can divide into groups. One group is the House of Representatives, another group is the Senate. A third group is the president and his or her advisors; another is "the people."

Now select someone to introduce the bill you want to present, and move it through the process. This might make it easier to learn all the steps. You will also understand how complicated it is to pass a new law. Design a bill concerning something you care about very much, perhaps something like pollution, or gun control, or some health concern.

- A bill is introduced in the House of Representatives and is placed in a basket known as the *hopper*.

- The bill is read (by title only) by the Clerk of the House, and it is assigned a number and ordered to be printed.

- The Speaker of the House (a member chosen by the others to be the presiding officer) refers the printed bill to a committee which studies it. Some committee meetings are public (called *open hearings*), and others are private.

- The committee may report the bill favorably, or amend (change) it, revise it, rewrite it, or *table* it (forget it unless it is reintroduced by a later congress).

- If they approve the bill, it is put on the House calendar to await its turn for consideration by the full House. If the bill is an emergency measure, or concerns a very important matter, the House Rules Committee has the power to push it ahead of others.

- After reaching the "floor" of the House (where the members meet), the bill is read again in full. Congressmen and congresswomen study it and speak for or against it.

- The bill may be amended or returned to committee for revision before a vote is taken in the full House.

- The House votes on the bill. If the majority votes for the bill, it comes to a third reading (this one by title only), and another vote is taken.

- If the bill passes the House, it is sent to the Senate.

- The Senate clerk reads it (by title).

- The vice-president (who presides over the Senate) assigns the bill to a senate committee for study. Again, the committee meetings may be open or closed to the public.

- The bill is filed and put on the Senate Calendar to wait its turn, or it is pushed ahead if it is important.

- The bill is read in full on the Senate floor. It is debated without a time limit (unless a limit is imposed) and brought to a vote.

- If it is passed, it is read a third time (by title) and put to another vote.

- If it is passed again, it is sent to the vice-president for signing. (The vice-president of the United States is the same person who presides over the Senate.)

- If the Senate amends (changes) a bill, it is returned to the House of Representatives for approval or further revision.

- If the House does not approve these changes, a conference committee composed of members of both houses meet to work out their differences.

- When there is agreement, the bill is sent back to the House and Senate for final approval.

- After Congress has signed the bill it is sent to the president for signing.

- If the president signs the bill, it becomes a law.

- If the president does not sign it, but does nothing for ten days (excluding Sundays), the bill becomes a law without his or her signature. This is called a *pocket veto*. The president does not give approval by signing, but the bill becomes a law. A pocket veto can also happen if the president receives the bill when less than ten days are left before Congress adjourns, and does nothing about the bill.

- If the president does not want the bill, he or she can veto it and send it back to Congress. A veto is a "no" vote. Congress can override this veto, but only with a two-thirds majority vote in both houses.

Fractured Fairytales

Okay, you legal eagles, now is a good time to see if you would like to spend your life in a law-related job. How about developing the following cases? For definitions that might help you consider charges, refer to the section on crimes in Chapter 10, "When People Break the Law."

In an earlier chapter I presented the "facts of a case" and asked how you would proceed if you were the district attorney. Now that you have come this far in the book you should have enough facts to assume many roles in thinking through an alleged crime.

Even though you are pretty old to think about fairytales, they have some challenging plots in terms of legal behavior. (Actually they are bounced around law schools all the time.) I am sure if you start with some of these, and perhaps consider some of today's movies as well, you will be able to experience many roles in the justice system. Look at each event as if you were a police officer or sheriff, as a judge, an attorney for either side, or as a citizen.

Analyze the following stories and look for criminal behavior.

Snow White	Cinderella
Jack and the Beanstalk	Red Riding Hood
Rumplestiltskin	Hansel and Gretel

The Three Pigs and the Big Bad Wolf

How about Peter Pan or the Exterminator, or Rambo, or . . .

Judge for Yourself

The following little scenes or situations are for you to consider in terms of all this new legal thinking we have developed. On pages 50 to 54 is a list of actions that are criminal and punishable.

These scenes are really parts of stories which do not have endings. The scenes involve people, their actions, and some of the things that happen or could happen because of these actions.

So you think it might be fun to be a lawyer, maybe even a judge—well, judge for yourself!

Think of what legal actions could take place. Think of civil law suits that could arise. Think of responsibility, and who might be involved even if they had nothing to do directly with the people starting the suit. Think of words like judgment, culpability (who gets or shares the blame), negligence (not doing something you should do).

There are many roles for you to assume. You can read these as judge, jury, prosecutor, defendant, and so forth. I hope these stories and questions stimulate some great discussions with your friends and classmates. For the best answers you might want to ask some experts. Some questions might not have just one easy answer. Try this one—

The Case of the Man and the Dog

> A man is walking on the sidewalk and a little yappy dog runs from its yard and nips at the man's ankle. The man gives the dog a hard kick. The owner of the dog comes running out of his house and is furious. He is a big fellow and beats the man who kicked his dog. Really beats him badly! Was any crime committed? Sort out the facts.

Suppose the owner of the dog was a karate champion and could really hurt someone seriously? If someone is a karate champion, is that person a lethal or dangerous weapon? Suppose there was a leash law, and it was against the law for the dog to be outside without a leash. Is the dog guilty? Can a dog be guilty? Was the man who kicked the dog justified? Was it cruelty to an animal? Was it self-defense? Who is guilty of what? Is anyone guilty of assault? Were any laws broken? Can anyone sue the other? Judge for yourself. Would you like to be on a jury that might have to hear a case like this?

The Case of the Building that Fell Down
This one is really complicated, but don't get discouraged.

> A business wanted a new office building. They asked several contractors to send in bids to do the construction work. To send in a bid means that the contractors will state what they will do and how much it will cost to do the job. Often the company with the lowest bid will get the contract.

Okay, Mr. Jones gets the contract. While the job is going along, Mr. Jones thinks he can save some money, so he uses less steel and makes a cheaper cement. The building looks beautiful and everyone is happy. Two years later there is an earthquake. It is not a very big quake, and most buildings do well, but the one Mr. Jones built has a great deal of damage. In fact the walls collapse. To add to the trouble, one of the people in the building has a heart attack and dies.

Okay, all you legal wizards, think! Is Mr. Jones responsible for the building collapsing? Was that earthquake a true test of the safety of the building, or was it a freak of nature that nobody could have prevented? Was Mr. Jones responsible for the woman's heart attack? Whether there was a legal responsibility or not, was there a moral responsibility? That means owing more than just the limits of the law—owing the decent, humane, special attention to your job or responsibility.

Were safety standards met? If not, should the district attorney start criminal proceedings? If there is no criminal trial, can there be a civil suit? Could anyone sue someone else for damages? Could the family of the person who died sue anyone?

What about the company that had the building built? They paid the contractor and rented out the space to others. Are they responsible? Did they hire that contractor because they thought he was good, or did they know he "cut the standards" so they wouldn't have to pay so much? Should the construction industry group that sets the standards punish the construction company with a fine or by taking away their license?

This is a very complicated case that would have adults arguing in court for years. There is no yes-or-no, black-or-white answer. The facts are not clear. This would be a hard one for a jury. Much of their decision would be based on opinion. The attorneys would be trying to suggest or form that opinion for members of the jury.

I hope you see why it is important not to make hasty judgments, why it is important to consider all the facts and to respect others who might not think the same as you. Much to think about.

The Case of the Child Who Drove a Car

> A child saw an empty automobile with the keys in it. He got in and drove it away. He raced along and didn't hit anything, but he caused a blue car to swerve and it hit a red car. The police chased the car with the child driving, and it ended up in someone's yard. Luckily it stopped before it hit the house, but it did hit a tree. The driver of the red car was injured. The grass in front of the house was really torn up. The car the child was driving was damaged when it hit the tree. The child broke his nose.

First, can you separate the criminal law issues from the civil issues? Were any laws broken? Were any laws broken? Can the driver of the red car sue anyone? If he has auto insurance and the driver of the blue car has auto insurance, what do you think the insurance companies will do? What about the child? What about his parents? Are they responsible for anything? Can a car left unlocked with the key in the ignition be considered a public nuisance?

Take this as far as you can. I am not going to give you many hints, but pretend you are the district attorney first. Then think as if you are the parents of the child. Should you sue anybody? What would you do if you were the owners of the cars?

The Case of the Faulty Watch
This is a short, rather neat one.

> A woman bought a watch. The watch didn't work right, and she missed her airplane. That meant that she missed an important meeting and didn't get a contract, and so her company lost a good deal of money.

Can she sue the company that made the watch? Can she sue the company that sold the watch? Can she sue the person that sold the watch to her? Even if you decide that the woman can sue someone, another thought is, *should* she sue? If you think she can, should she sue for a new watch, or for all the money she and her company would have made if she had gotten the contract?

Would it make a difference if the watch cost $10,000? If the watch cost $12 and had a guarantee, would you think differently than if the watch cost $1,000 and did not have a guarantee? This time be one of the jurors. Can you separate the facts from how you feel?

The Case of the Fainting Burglar
This is a real situation that happened recently.

> A burglar broke into a dentist's office. He was looking for drugs, money, and dental gold. He really trashed the office looking around and cut himself badly on some glass he broke. He fainted and was later found there by the police.

Since he never got out of the office with whatever he wanted to steal, on what charges do you think the police could arrest him—if any?

Could the burglar sue the dentist for the damage he suffered when he cut himself? Could the dentist sue the burglar? Does it make a difference to you that the dentist is wealthy and the burglar is poor?

In the real situation, the burglar did sue the dentist, and he won an award of money. The jury felt the dentist was wealthy and was insured so it wouldn't cost the dentist anything. The burglar was poor and the jury thought it would be nice if he got something. Was this a just decision?

Please think about insurance companies and about juries which award huge damages believing that these companies can pay any award without hurting anyone. Juries very often will make awards if they feel some business will pay it. Actually, insurance companies pass along the loss by raising the cost of insurance to you.

This is a good time to think about the words justice, judgment, and responsibility. It is also a good time to remember that we need intelligent, fair, honest people to serve on juries. Often busy men and women try to get out of jury duty. You must think of what kind of jurors you would want if you went on trial. I wonder if that dentist will be anxious to serve on a jury if he is called.

The Case of the Baby Swing
This is a case that involves insurance—the kind called product liability insurance.

> A woman bought a baby swing. While her child was in this swing it broke, and the baby fell to the ground. The baby was hurt.

Think about the idea of responsibility. What responsibility does the store that sold the swing have? What responsibility does the manufacturer have?

Now go back further and think what responsibility does the company who made the metal parts have? If the parents of the baby sue, who do you think they will name in the suit? If the case goes to trial, they might call in expert witnesses, people who might point out how the swing failed. Was the failure in how the swing was put together? Was the failure in the metal that supported the weight of the child? Was the failure in the directions for assembling the swing? Was the swing recommended for children of a certain size or weight? Are there any criminal aspects to the case? On and on the witnesses could go. The jurors would have much to think about.

The Case of the Guns at the Gas Station

John drove to the service station to pump some gas. When his tank was filled he started to drive away without paying. The owner of the station ran over to block the path of the car and stopped John. The owner told him that he was breaking the law and he, the owner, was going to call the police.

John panicked and picked up a gun he had lying on the seat beside him. When the owner saw the gun he feared for his life. He reached into his jacket and pulled out his gun and shot John. John died. Later the police found that John's gun was not loaded.

Is the owner guilty of murder, or was this self-defense? If you were the district attorney, would you charge the owner with murder 1, murder 2, or manslaughter—or would you charge him at all? If a district attorney does bring charges, a criminal trial might result.

There could also be a civil lawsuit, which might result in a civil trial. Suppose John's family sues the owner of the service station for depriving them of a loved one who was also the wage-earner in the family. Now you are on the jury. Would you award John's family any money? If you do, the owner of the station would have to pay it. Does the fact that John's gun was not loaded mean the owner acted without cause?

The Case of the Tall Ladder

Mary was having her roof repaired. The "roofer" (the person who does the work) put a tall ladder up against the house. He needed more nails and drove off to the store to get them. He left the ladder where it was because he was coming right back.

Some teenagers were playing ball next door. Suddenly the ball went over the fence and landed on Mary's roof. One of the teenagers climbed up the ladder, got on the roof, fell, and died.

What a grim story. The teen's parents wanted the roofer to be charged with murder for leaving the ladder where it was a temptation to a minor. If you were the district attorney would you find sufficient cause to charge the man with murder?

If there is a criminal trial, would it matter that the boy was a teenager and not a five-year-old? Does being a teenager mean that more good judgment is expected? If the ladder is a temptation for a five-year-old, but no little child climbed it, is the roofer more or less guilty? Does the roofer's intent matter? (Did he plan a murder, or was he just being lazy or reckless?)

How would you respond if you were the district attorney? How would you respond if you were defending the roofer? How would you vote if you were on that jury? I hope you wouldn't vote on such scanty information. You might have an opinion with the little information I gave to you, but you would also need many more facts, good evidence, and instructions from a judge before you make such an important decision.

Now let's think about civil law. Can the teen's parents sue the roofer? If the roofer has no money, can they then sue Mary because it was her roof?

What does the word ac*cident* mean? Is someone always responsible for an accident? Should anyone be sued? In our country people often see a lawsuit as a way to get "easy" money. Many companies go out of business because they are held responsible for an action of one of their workers.

The Case of the Deadly Hamburger

Paul Brown ordered a hamburger in a fast-food restaurant. Shortly after eating it he became very ill and died. At the autopsy (a medical examination to find out why a person has died) it was found that the hamburger contained sharp pieces of bone which damaged Paul's stomach.

First, pretend you are the district attorney. Something went wrong. This shouldn't have happened. Was there any criminal action?

There are many regulations in the meat-packing business. There are standards that must be met, by law. Will you do an investigation? If the meat packers have broken the law, will you prosecute? And who will you find *at fault* (to blame)? Was it the fault of the meat-packing company or of a worker who was sloppy? Will you charge the president of the meat-packing business with murder? If you can find the meat inspector, will you hold him or her responsible? Or is anyone responsible? How would you go about proving who did what? What about the cook? Is he or she responsible for anything?

Suppose Paul's parents decide to sue someone. They might first try the owner of the restaurant. This would probably be the easiest thing to do, because the restaurant is right in town. They know the owner's name and they think he has plenty of money and insurance.

Let's say the Browns start a lawsuit against the restaurant, and their attorney hires an investigator who finds out where the restaurant buys its meat. Now they can consider suing whoever sold the meat. Suppose the investigator finds out that the meat was mixed with the bone at the meat-packing plant. Should they sue the meat-packing plant??

A very big question is: Just because something terrible happened, should people automatically sue anyone or everyone?

A few more questions. If any of these people lose a lawsuit, should they sue their attorneys for malpractice (that means not doing their job well)? Because Paul died, should his parents sue the doctor for malpractice? Was the doctor at fault simply because he was Paul's doctor and Paul didn't get better? Many people think a doctor is wrong if a patient dies for any reason. They do not like to consider that each person's body reacts differently, and not everyone responds perfectly to surgery, medicines, or other treatment.

More To Think About

It might be interesting to read over some of these cases again, pretending that you are one of the attorneys. Prepare your case. Who would you call as witnesses? Plan to win! Then, suddenly become an attorney for the other side. Can you fight just as earnestly to win for this other side?

I hope you enjoyed considering these cases. If you want more to discuss and think about, just read your newspaper. Daily there are stories of things happening to people throughout the paper, from the front page to the sports section.

Being a Witness

In Chapter 13 I described the duties of a trial witness. I shall repeat just a little bit here, but will also tell you more about our senses and our powers of observation—powers that we must use when we are a witness.

A witness in court testifies (tells under oath) what he has seen or heard or felt or smelled or tasted. He must recall what he has experienced with his senses.

The Sense of Sight

Eyes: With our two eyes we can quickly observe details of what is happening close to us or far away. Our eyes work with our brain to give us information. We learn to judge shape, distance, motion, and so on with surprising accuracy.

We use these judgments over and over until they become automatic, yet sometimes that judgment proves to be wrong and what we think we saw might not be the same as what the eye saw. In a case like that, what we think we saw is called an *illusion*. There is no clear line between illusion and reality, and we constantly make small corrections in judgment. We do this without knowing it. Some illusions are so strong that it is hard to see things as they really are.

An *optical illusion* involves the use of our eyes—our sight. I'll give you some well-known optical illusions. Look at them and test your perception. Don't forget! To be a witness you must be positive about what you say you have seen. Look at the figures shown on the next page. These are examples of the eye seeing one thing and the mind making judgments based on what it perceived. We make other judgments based on other clues to the brain.

If we are talking about distance and proportion, the apparent size of an object depends on the distance it is from the observer.

> A ball held close to the eye will appear large. If you hold the same ball far away it will appear small. The same is true of what seems to be the size of the sun and moon. The sun is much larger than the moon, but they seem about the same size because the moon is closer to us and the sun is farther away.

All the information about the size of things around us gives our brain clues to judge distance. Objects close to us partially overlap those that are far away.

> Look at something far away—such as a car down the street. Now hold your hand up fairly close to your eyes. Your hand is covering the car. The car even seems much smaller than your hand. Your brain has to take in other clues to let you know that your hand is not really larger than that car. That is perception.

Objects farther away seem to fade or be a lighter color. They lose contrast.

> Mountains farthest away are lighter or paler than the mountains in front.

If the observer is moving—for instance, riding in a car, objects close to the car will look like they are moving much more quickly than objects further away.

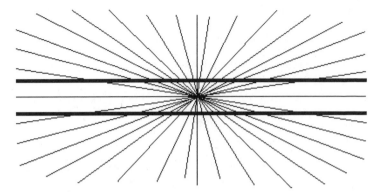

Are the dark lines straight or curved?

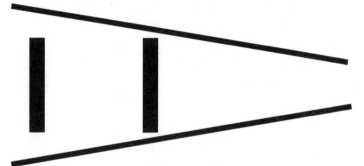

Which stick is taller?

Are the inside squares the same size?

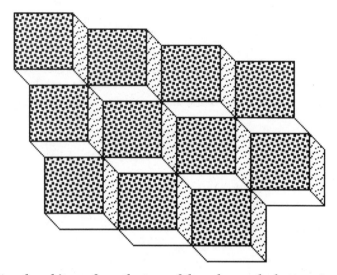

Are the white surfaces the tops of the cubes or the bottoms?

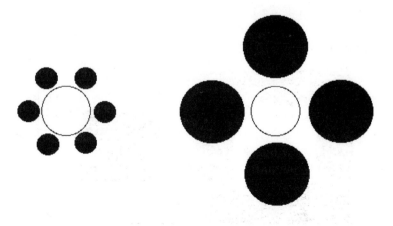

Which of the white circles is larger?

> When you are looking out of the car window and the car
> is moving, the mountains or the moon or the sun will not
> seem to move very much at all. Yet the telephone poles
> or parked cars at the curb, or people walking, seem to
> be moving much faster. They whiz past us. Again, our
> brain must use many clues to make the right judgment of
> distance and speed.

All this is rather amazing, isn't it? Actually you are a rather
amazing person with a definitely amazing body. Use it well.

The Sense of Touch

Another sense that we might use as a witness is the sense of
touch. Our skin has "receptors" that make us sensitive to
different pressures. These receptors are like threads which
send clues to the brain. We use these messages to keep us in
touch with where we are and with what we are in contact.

With the sense of touch we can feel the difference between
cold and hot. We can tell if an object is smooth or rough. We
can tell if something is large or small, heavy or light, tall or
short. If you are told you are holding something made of
paper, you expect it to be lighter than an object made of iron.
This is some of the information in our brain that we have
already learned. We can judge whether this paper object is
lighter than expected or heavier than expected. We can make
a judgment.

You can make some interesting tests of your sense of touch.
If you are touched quickly with something very, very cold and
something hot, you might have trouble telling the difference. If
you are handed a long, slimy "thing," you might have trouble
telling whether it is a worm or some wet spaghetti. (Of course
you could always use your sense of taste and test it that way—
if you are brave enough or foolish enough.)

> In court it would not be hard to give your opinion that a
> thing was soft or hard, smooth or rough, cold or hot. I
> used the word *opinion* because all of these judgments

could be followed with the question: "How?" How smooth, or how hot, or how soft?

As a juror in a criminal trial, you must be sure "without a reasonable doubt." As a witness you need to be that sure also.

The Sense of Hearing

Our sense of hearing also gives clues to our brain. Sounds that are high or low, soft or loud, sharp or soft, help us to form judgments. If we hear a scream we can often tell if it is a scream of pain or fear or even happy excitement. A whisper is certainly different from shouting. Laughing is certainly differ-ent from crying. We can often judge distance by how loud or how soft a sound is.

> When cars pass quickly past us we hear a whizzing sound. Footsteps can tell us how far or how fast or how boldly or how secretly a person is moving. We can even tell the difference between something hitting wood or glass or metal.

If you are a witness, you must not give your opinion, but only the facts. For instance, it would not be correct to say the person was angry because you heard him stomping around. It would be correct to describe the sound you heard, such as stomping and stamping. But on the witness stand you may not draw the logical conclusion that he was angry. Even though you might have heard a scream that sounded like someone was frightened, you must only describe the scream and not draw the conclusion.

With your class or some friends, try experimenting with sound. It is amazing how closing our eyes affects how we hear—and even what we hear. It would seem funny to test your hearing by blindfolding your eyes. Yet after ten or more minutes you will be much more sensitive about how far away sounds are, what actions you can hear, and how you will judge what people are doing.

The Sense of Smell

Our noses sense the difference between a sweet smell or a stinky smell. We use this sense to tell the brain that something is burning, and whether that burning smell is a barbecue or a house on fire. Good smells like cooking food and bad smells like burning food are easy for us to sense. But this judgment happens after the clues reach the brain.

We are lucky to have a sharp sense of smell, or we would have many accidents. Imagine what would happen if gasoline smelled the same as milk, or if peanut butter smelled like ground onions.

If you were to give testimony in court, you might be able to say what a certain smell made you think of, but unless it was a common smell, such as a wood fire or gasoline or chocolate, your judgment could be questioned. It is hard to be exact in describing smells, because there are not many words to describe them. If I asked you to describe a smell, the first word you might use is the word *like*. You know, "Well, it smelled *like* a flower," or "It smelled *like* a wet dog," or it smelled like something sour or sweet.

Try to detect different smells while you are blindfolded. You might be surprised to find that your nose is a pretty good detective.

A Witness Needs More than the Senses

Even if all your senses are working well, does that mean you would be a good witness? The answer would depend on how observing you really are, how well you can remember what you experienced, and how well you can tell the jury or judge exactly what you mean to say.

> If the lawyer asks you what color socks the man had on, or whether he had lots of hair on the top of his head, you can only tell what you saw. If you were lying on the floor, maybe you had a good look at the person's socks but couldn't see the top of his head. If you were atop a tall

ladder you might have seen the top of his head. A witness can only testify to what he actually saw.

Try looking at news photographs of an accident. Examine the pictures for three minutes and then cover them up. Now start telling what you saw to classmates or other people you are with. Listen to what the others think they saw. Then come back the next day and swear that you will answer accurately and truthfully when someone asks you questions about the scene of the accident. How accurately are you able to remember what happened?

Or have a small group enact a crime, with another group looking on. The "actors" should set out some props, wear clothing that can be identified, and create some confusing, noisy happening. This should take only a few seconds and then they should disappear. Twenty minutes later, the group that observed the scene should be questioned, one at a time, so they won't copy what others said. It will be interesting to see what each will remember.

Being a good witness begins to seem complicated, doesn't it? Actually you are probably a better witness than you think. Just keep alert. And remember: a witness must be able to observe, recall, and relate.

Freedomland

In this book's chapters on the U.S. Constitution and the amendments, we quote thousands of words about the rights of citizens. It can be easy to lose your way in all these words, and they may have little meaning until you need to claim one of these rights. I think it will be more meaningful if you try doing the same thing our early leaders did. I mean, try to form a new nation with its own constitution. Let's give it a name, like Freedomland.

Now to begin! Remember, you must not do this alone. If you did this alone you would be a dictator, or you could just declare yourself king or queen. You must work in a group of friends or classmates.

Just so you won't design a government that gives all the power to yourself, you will have to submit this new constitution to the people in Freedomland for their vote. So you'd better find out their concerns and see if you can satisfy them.

This nation, Freedomland, is filled with all kinds of people from many different places. Many of these people are rich and many are poor. Some have no education and can barely read or write, while others are highly educated. Now your job is to create some form of government that will let each person live with as much liberty and justice as possible. I suppose you will want to have some kind of meeting or convention so representatives (delegates) from the people can work together. When you select delegates, remember that they should represent all the people. These delegates probably should have a good education and should be able to think clearly and fairly, and should really care.

Pretend that you are one of the delegates to the convention. And remember that since you are representing others, you might have to report back to them at different times. You might even want to get advice or permission from some. For example if you were representing a large group of farmers in your colony, you would want to know what their concerns were.

Each of you probably wants some special freedom first. You can get some hints by seeing the way the United States government began, and you can judge if the men who wrote the Constitution did a good job. The U.S. Constitution is not perfect. The framers of this wonderful document never expected perfection. They knew that people would disagree even if they were good, intelligent, and honorable citizens. They also knew that time would bring changes, so they made room for these changes by allowing amendments. As we saw in Chapter 17, the first ten amendments are called the Bill of Rights. This is the most powerful protection of individual freedom ever written.

It will be interesting to see if you will come up with fewer amendments to your constitution, or will add more.

In designing a constitution, remember that you are not setting up a list of laws. Your lawmakers are supposed to do that. You are setting up a list of guarantees of rights and protections—the rights and protection of individual persons from all other people and from the government itself.

You are designing a government, and your constitution will perhaps tell your government what it cannot do and what it must do to allow all of you to live with as much personal freedom as possible. You want this government to represent all your citizens; to guarantee them the freedoms they deserve, the freedoms stated in the Declaration of Independence, which can be had in a government of all the people, for the people, and by the people.

Before you start writing, perhaps you should consider a few things, such as:

- Is Freedomland made of smaller states?

- If so, are those states all the same, or do some have big business centers where the economy of the land is decided?

- Do certain other states contain most of the farms that feed this country?

- How will you get money to run this new nation?

- Who will be the leader, and how will he or she get the job of leading?

- Who will make the laws?

- Who will carry these laws out?

- What do you do about people moving from other countries to this new land?

• Should this constitution cover every aspect of
living, or should it be just a guideline?

There are lots of things to consider to set up a government
that is strong and will still treat all people as equal.

Our U.S. Constitution started with a preamble which stated
its goals. Perhaps that is where you should start. It would be
helpful to review the seven basic articles of the Constitution
now (page 120). Then you can assign different persons to
different aspects of this new government. Some can establish
the branches of government. Others, perhaps, will concern
themselves with civil rights, or the environment, or women's
issues, outer space, defense, taxes, or any of the big issues
that are important today. Good luck!

GLOSSARY

ACCUSATORY PROCESS. Under United States criminal law, this is the process whereby we accuse someone of a deed and then must prove it.

ABDUCT. To carry away by force a wife or child or ward. The unlawful detention of a female.

ABET. To incite or encourage someone to commit a crime.

ABSCOND. To go secretly out of a court's jurisdiction or to hide within the jurisdiction in order to avoid legal proceeding.

ACCESSORY. A person who is involved, either before or after, in the commission of a felony. That person does not necessarily have to be present at the deed.

ACCOMPLICE. A person who participates in the commission of a crime, either as the offender or a helper.

ACQUIT. To release or discharge from a liability, obligation, or engagement. To release from a criminal charge.

ADJOURNMENT. The act of putting off, postponing, or suspending business or a session.

ADMIRALTY LAW. The branch of law that deals with maritime affairs, both civil and criminal. Maritime affairs have to do with the sea. Admiralty law is the law of the sea and is handled by federal courts.

ADOPTION. Voluntarily taking a child into one's family and giving him or her all the rights, privileges, and duties of one's own child. An adoption must be authorized by the court according to state law.

AGENT. A person who is authorized by another to act for him.

ALIBI. A Latin word meaning "elsewhere." In criminal prosecution, an alibi is a defense by which the accused establishes or attempts to establish his innocence by showing that he was elsewhere than at the scene of the crime when it was committed.

ALLEGATION. The formal written statement by a person in a legal action, telling what he expects to prove in the case, whether for the plaintiff or for the defense.

ALTERNATE JURORS. People selected to serve on the jury if any juror is unable to complete service. An alternate juror is sworn in and sits through the trial and is prepared to act as a juror.

AMENDMENT. The act of altering (changing) or modifying a law, bill, or motion. The correction of an error or defect in any process, pleading, or proceeding at law.

AMICUS CURIAE. A Latin term that means "a friend of the court" (one not a party in the action). In law, often means a person who volunteers information on the law or facts of a case.

APPEAL. A request that a judgment be reviewed by a higher court.

ARBITRATION. A form of settling a dispute in which the parties bring their dispute (disagreement) to a neutral third party for a decision.

ARRAIGNMENT. In a criminal case, the proceeding in which an accused person is brought before a judge to hear the charges against him or her and to enter a plea of guilty or not guilty. Also called a preliminary hearing or initial appearance.

ARREST. To take into custody by a law-enforcement officer.

ARSON. The malicious setting fire to another person's property. Originally the only property involved in arson was a dwelling (the building in which someone lives). Statutes in many states make arson also the burning of buildings other than dwellings. It is not arson to burn your own building—that is a different offense.

ARTICULABLE FACTS. Facts that can be told clearly, as when establishing probable cause for an arrest.

ASSAULT. The intentional display of force that would give the victim reason to fear bodily harm, or the actual use of force to carry out this threat.

ATTORNEY-CLIENT PRIVILEGE. Communication made in confidence between an attorney and client is protected. The attorney does not have to tell about any information disclosed by the client relating to representations.

BAIL.   Money or other security given to secure a person's release from custody. The judge decides whether the accused be allowed to post bail. If the person does not show up for trial after being released on bail, he can be arrested and the bail is forfeited. If the person does show up, the bail will be handed back.

BAIL BOND.   The obligation or pledge signed by the accused to secure his presence at trial.

BAILIFF.   A courtroom security officer. He or she could be a sheriff, a marshal, or any other court attendant who takes charge of the defendant, guards the jury, keeps order in the courtroom, and performs other duties for the court.

BAR.   Historically a partition separating the general public from the space occupied by the judge, lawyers, and other participants in a trial. The term is now used when referring to lawyers.

BATTERY.   The unlawful use of force by one person on another.

BEYOND A REASONABLE DOUBT.   The standard of proof in a criminal case requiring a jury (or judge in a case that is tried without a jury) to be satisfied to a moral certainty that every element of the crime has been proved by the prosecution in order to find the defendant guilty.

BIGAMY.   The crime of a person who marries more than one person without ever dissolving his or her other marriages.

BOOKING.   The process of photographing, fingerprinting, and recording other identifying data of a suspect following arrest.

BREACH OF CONTRACT.   A legally inexcusable failure to perform a contract.

BRIBERY.   The crime of giving or offering something of value to try to influence the action of a person in some official public position.

BURDEN OF PROOF.   The necessity of proving facts or issues in dispute. The party who accuses another carries the burden of proof and must prove that certain facts are true in order to prevail in the lawsuit. In a criminal trial this burden is the responsibility of the prosecution. In a civil trial it is the responsibility of the plaintiff.

BURGLARY.   The crime of unlawfully and intentionally breaking in and entering a dwelling with the intent to commit a felony. Some states have expanded the definition to include entering any building, not just a dwelling (where someone lives).

CAPITAL CRIME. A crime punishable by death.

CASE LAW. Law developed through case decisions. Attorneys will cite (refer to) other cases to plead their case.

CERTIORARI. A procedure for bringing a case before a higher court.

CHANGE OF VENUE. Moving a lawsuit to another place for trial.

CHILD ABUSE. The act of willfully causing or permitting a child to suffer needlessly, or inflicting unjustifiable physical or mental suffering, or having the care or custody of any child and willfully causing or permitting the child to be placed in peril.

CIRCUMSTANTIAL EVIDENCE. Evidence that does not directly prove the allegation or charge, but gives enough indirect facts that the jury will think it reasonable to assume the allegation or charge is true.

CIVIL ACTION. A noncriminal case in which one person or entity sues another for compensation or a redress of private or civil rights.

CLEMENCY. An act by the president or governor to ease or lessen the consequences (the sentence) from a criminal act or conviction. It must take the form of a commutation (this usually means lowering the sentence) or a pardon.

CLERK OF THE COURT. The clerk is a public official who keeps on file the court records, such as the docket (list of cases waiting to be heard). Other duties may include issuing summons, swearing in the jury, the witnesses, and the bailiff, entering evidence in the trial record, reading the verdict, or issuing the judgment.

CLOSING ARGUMENTS. The final statements by the attorneys to the jury before deliberating, summing up the trial, testimony, and evidence.

COMMON LAW. A system of law in which rulings are determined by legal precedents rather than the legislative law. See also CASE LAW.

COMPLAINT. The legal document that begins a lawsuit. In the complaint the plaintiff alleges the facts on which the lawsuit is based and identifies the action the court is asked to take.

COMPLAINANT. The party who complains or sues, one who applies to the court for legal redress. The plaintiff.

CONCURRENT SENTENCE. The sentence imposed on a convicted person when the sentences for more than one violation are to be served at the same time.

CONFIDENTIALITY. Treating information as private and not to be made public.

CONFLICT OF INTEREST. A lawyer shall not represent one client if by doing so it would create a problem for another of his clients, unless both clients consent and the lawyer truly believes that neither of them will be badly affected.

CONSECUTIVE SENTENCES. Sentences imposed on a person convicted of more than one crime or violation, which are to be served one after another.

CONTEMPT OF COURT. Willful disobedience of a court order.

CONTINUANCE. Postponement of a legal proceeding to a later date.

CONTRACT. A legally enforceable spoken or written agreement between two persons.

CONVICTION. A judgment of guilt against a criminal defendant.

COPYRIGHT. An author's legal right to protect what he or she has created.

COUNTERFEITING. To copy, imitate, or forge with the intent to pass it off as genuine or real or the original. This crime often involves the attempt to make imitation copies of paper money to cheat.

COURT CALENDAR. The schedule of hearings, trials, and other court procedures.

COURT REPORTER. A stenographer who takes every word of testimony, arguments, and judicial rulings and procedures during a trial.

CRIME. An act or omission (failure to act) in violation of public law which either forbids you to do the act or commands you to do it (such as demanding that you get a driver's license before you drive). Almost all crimes fall into two categories, felonies (very serious) or misdemeanors (less serious). Crimes are punishable and leave a criminal record. See pages 50 to 54 for a list of crimes with their definitions.

CRIMINAL LAW. The laws that we are commanded to obey, which deal with actions that are harmful to society (crimes).

CROSS-EXAMINATION. The questioning of a witness who was introduced by the other side in a legal proceeding.

DAMAGES. Money awarded by a court to a person, group, or business injured by the act of another.

DECISION. The judgment of a court of law.

DEFAULT. A failure to respond to a lawsuit within the specified time.

DEFENDANT. A person or entity (such as a business or corporation) named in a civil lawsuit, or accused of breaking the law.

DEPOSITION. The testimony of a witness taken under oath in preparation for a trial. It is a form of "discovery."

DIRECT EVIDENCE. An eyewitness account of something that was seen or experienced by the witness.

DIRECT EXAMINATION. The initial questioning of witnesses by the party for whom they are called. If you are subpoenaed to be a witness ant testify in court, the direct examination will be conducted by the attorney who called you.

DISCOVERY. The pretrial process by which the parties request from each other information about the evidence that will be relied upon at trial.

DISMISSAL. An order or judgment ending a lawsuit without a trial of the issues involved.

DISTURBING THE PEACE. Any willful act that unreasonably disturbs the public or tends strongly to create a disturbance is a breach of the peace which peace officers are sworn to uphold. In some states it is called disorderly conduct. For law enforcement, this is a really hard violation to define, and for the accused, it is hard to defend.

DOCKET. A list of the cases to be heard by a court. The court's official calendar of pending cases.

DOE. Defendants who are named in a suit, but are referred to as "Doe" because their names are unknown at the time of pleading. Often an unknown person is referred to as "Jane Doe" or "John Doe."

DOUBLE JEOPARDY. Putting a person on trial more than once for the same charge or crime. This is forbidden in the Fifth Amendment of the U.S. Constitution.

DUE PROCESS OF LAW. The rights and safeguards of the law and judicial process guaranteed to all persons by the U.S. Constitution.

EMBEZZLEMENT. The crime of taking money or goods for his own use by a person to whom these things have been entrusted, such as an agent who is to hold your money or invest it for you and who cheats and keeps some for himself.

EQUAL PROTECTION OF THE LAW. The guarantee in the Fourteenth Amendment to the U.S. Constitution that all people shall be treated equally by the law.

EQUITY. Justice or fairness.

ESTATE.   A person's property. If it is property in buildings and land it is called real property or real estate.

ET AL.   A Latin phrase for "and others," which is used to indicate additional parties in a case or suit.

EX POST FACTO.   Translated from the Latin, "after the fact." The Constitution prohibits the enactment of ex-post-facto laws. This means that a person cannot be convicted of an unlawful act if the act was made unlawful after the person committed it. If you drove a car sixty miles an hour on Monday, and it became illegal to drive faster than fifty-five miles an hour on Friday, you couldn't be arrested for what you did on the Monday before.

EXHIBIT.   A document or other object introduced as evidence in a trial or hearing.

EXPERT WITNESS.   A person with expertise in a specific field or area of study that is pertinent to a trial. Expert witnesses can be called to testify for either side in a lawsuit.

EXTORTION.   The crime of unlawfully obtaining money or something of value from a person by frightening the victim by violence, threat, or abuse of authority.

EXTRADITION.   The process by which one state surrenders, or gives up to another state, a person accused or convicted of a crime in that other state.

FELONY.   A crime that is of a grave (most serious) nature (not misdemeanors). Felonies are usually punishable by imprisonment in a state or federal prison or penitentiary for more than a year and/or by large fines.

FOREMAN OR FOREWOMAN.   The chairperson in a jury, who organizes discussion and conducts voting. He or she hands the verdict to the bailiff when ready.

FORGERY.   The crime of making a false document that looks like or copies a real document, legal form, check, or signature with the intent to defraud or cheat. It can also be the altering of any writing that, if genuine, would have a legal effect or be the foundation for a legal liability.

FRAUD.   Intentional deception to deprive another person of a right. To deceive someone or to fool or confuse them by saying or doing something that is not true.

GUARDIANSHIP.   Legal right given to a person to be responsible for the food, housing, and other necessities of another person who is found to be incapable of providing these for himself or herself.

GRAND JURY.   A group of citizens, usually numbering twenty-three, who are called to assemble in private to hear and review the facts of an investigation, to hear the allegations of criminal acts, and to determine if there is sufficient cause to prosecute or continue with the investigation.

HABEAS CORPUS.   A writ ordering an official to bring a suspect before the court in order to decide if there is sufficient evidence to hold the person.

HEARSAY.   Evidence that is not within the personal knowledge of the witness, but told to the witness by a third party or stated in a document. Hearsay evidence is usually inadmissible in a trial.

HOMICIDE.   The killing of a human being by another person. See also MURDER.

HUNG JURY.   A jury that is unable to reach a unanimous verdict.

INDICTMENT.   An accusation by the grand jury charging a person with a crime.

INFRACTION.   A violation of law not punishable by imprisonment. Minor traffic violations are generally considered infractions and are usually punished by fines (at least the first time).

INJUNCTION.   An order by a court directing a party to do, or refrain from (stop) doing, a particular act.

JUDGMENT.   A final decision of the court resolving the dispute and determining the rights and obligations of the parties to a lawsuit.

JUDICIAL REVIEW.   Authority of a court to review the official actions of other branches of government.

JURISDICTION.   The geographic area in which a court has power, or the types of cases that court has the power to hear. This defines the difference between the U.S. Supreme Court, state supreme courts, federal courts, superior courts, municipal courts, justice courts, and so forth.

JURY INSTRUCTIONS.   The statement of guidelines and law given by the judge to the jury which they are to use in deciding the issues of fact while they are deliberating.

JUVENILE COURT LAW. The system of justice which provides for the protection and safety of the public and each minor under the jurisdiction of the juvenile court. The word minor is defined differently in each state, but usually means under the age of eighteen. Your local bar association can tell you how to find out about juvenile law in your area.

KIDNAPPING. The forceful taking of a person and the holding of that person against his will.

LARCENY. Obtaining property by fraud or deceit.

LENIENCY. A recommendation requested by the prosecution that a judge impose a light sentence in a criminal case.

LIBEL. Written words or pictures that falsely defame a person.

MAGISTRATE. A judge of a court of limited jurisdiction, such as a justice of the peace or a judge in a police court.

MANSLAUGHTER. The unlawful killing of another without intent to kill, either voluntarily or involuntarily.

MEDIATION. A form of resolving a dispute in which the parties bring their dispute or disagreement before a neutral third part in an attempt to reach a peaceful, legal settlement.

MIRANDA WARNING. The warning police are required to give a suspect in custody before questioning. It informs the suspect of his constitutional rights. Unless the warning has been given, the suspect's statements will not be accepted in a court of law.

MISDEMEANOR. A criminal offense less serious than a felony. It is generally punishable by a fine or limited jail term.

MISTRIAL. A trial that is ended before a verdict is reached, because of basic error before coming to trial, a hung jury, or some extraordinary circumstance.

MURDER. The unlawful killing of another with malice aforethought. This means the killing was planned ahead of the act.

NEGLIGENCE. Failure to exercise the degree of care that a reasonable person would exercise under the same circumstances.

NOLO CONTENDERE. A plea of No Contest in a criminal case. The defendant does not disagree with the charge, but does not plead "not guilty" to the charge. He accepts a sentence.

OPENING STATEMENT. The statement that each attorney makes to a jury as he outlines for them the charges in the trial and what he hopes to prove and what the evidence will show.

ORDINANCE. A law passed by a local government body such as a city council or county commission.

PAROLE. The supervised, conditional release of a prisoner before completion of his sentence. When a prisoner is released on parole he must keep in constant contact with his parole officer to assure he is obeying the conditions of his parole. The conditions are the rules he must obey.

PARTY. A person or entity (such as a company or corporation) involved in the prosecution or defense of a legal proceeding.

PATENT. The exclusive right that an inventor has to profit by his invention for a certain time.

PERJURY. The criminal offense of making a false statement under oath.

PLAINTIFF. The person who introduces or initiates a lawsuit.

PLEA. In a criminal proceeding, the defendant's answer in open court as to whether he is guilty or not guilty of the crime charged.

PLEA BARGAINING. The process of negotiation between the prosecutor and the defendant in which a settlement can be reached before or instead of a trial. For example, the defendant may be willing to plead guilty to a less serious offense in return for not being prosecuted for the original, more serious charge.

PRECEDENT. A previously decided case that guides the decisions of future cases. An attorney will "cite" (refer to) the previous case to help the judge make his decision.

PRELIMINARY HEARING. In criminal law, the hearing at which a judge determines whether there is sufficient evidence against a person charged with a crime to warrant holding him for trial.

PRETRIAL CONFERENCE. A meeting between the judge and lawyers involved in a lawsuit to define the issues and agree on what will be presented at trial. Usually a final effort is made to settle the case without a trial.

PRIMA FACIE CASE. A case for which sufficient evidence has been presented to justify a finding on behalf of the part presenting the case, if the other party's contradictory evidence is not considered.

PROBABLE CAUSE.   Sufficient legal reasons for allowing the search and seizure for evidence and/or the arrest of anyone. Often referred to as "sufficient cause."

PROBATION.   Suspending the sentence of a convicted offender and giving him freedom during good behavior under the supervision of a probation officer.

PROSECUTOR.   The lawyer representing the government in a criminal case (usually a district attorney in most state criminal cases). Federal courts have their own prosecutors.

PUBLIC DEFENDER.   A government lawyer who provides free legal defense services to persons charged with a crime who are unable to pay for a lawyer. If a town does not have a public defender, practicing attorneys from the town take turns serving in this role. Representation by an attorney is guaranteed in the Sixth Amendment to the U.S. Constitution.

RAPE.   The crime of sexual intercourse with a person without consent, usually by force or deception. Statutory Rape is any act of sexual intercourse with a person below the age of consent.

READINESS AND SETTLEMENT HEARING.   A conference (held instead of a jury trial) where both attorneys talk about the facts of a criminal case where the defendant has pleaded not guilty. They discuss the facts of the case, possible defenses, the defendant's prior record, and any other information that is important to the case. Together they work toward some solution that will satisfy the court. If satisfied, the judge then hands down the sentence based on these recommendations. Such hearings are usually for less serious offenses, such as misdemeanors.

REBUTTAL.   Evidence offered to disprove other evidence previously given.

RECORD.   A collection of all the documents and other evidence in a case.

RECEIVING STOLEN PROPERTY.   The crime of accepting property with the knowledge that it was unlawfully obtained such as by theft, extortion, embezzlement, etc., and with the intent of depriving the owner from getting it back—which is criminal intent. In most states this is a felony.

REDIRECT EXAMINATION.   The questioning of one side's own witness after cross-examination by the opposing party. If your attorney calls a witness for testimony and then the other side questions him, your attorney may ask that witness to clarify or explain what he just answered to the opposing side's attorney.

REST. A party, or side, in a trial is said to rest or to rest its case when it has presented all the evidence it intends to offer.

RIOT. A violent public disturbance.

ROBBERY. Taking another's property from his person or immediate space (the area near him) by force or threat.

SEARCH WARRANT. A written order issued by a judge (after he hears the "probable cause") that directs a law enforcement officer to search a specific area for a specific piece of evidence. This permission must be obtained before an officer can enter a person's space to search or seize. This is a protection of the Fourth Amendment to the U.S. Constitution.

SELF-DEFENSE. A claim that an act, which might be considered criminal, was justifiable because it was necessary to protect a person or property from another.

SELF-INCRIMINATION. Testimony that might prove you (the person giving the testimony) are guilty. The Constitution protects a person from self-incrimination in the Fifth Amendment. A person does not have to testify against himself. The burden of proof is on the prosecution.

SENTENCE. The penalty pronounced upon a person who has been convicted by due process of law in a criminal prosecution.

SETTLEMENT. An agreement between the parties disposing or ending a lawsuit.

SMALL CLAIMS COURT. A court that handles civil claims for small amounts of money.

STATUTORY LAW. Law enacted by the legislative branch of the government.

SUBPOENA. A court order compelling (making) a witness to appear and testify.

TESTIMONY. Evidence given by a witness under oath. This means that the witness has sworn to the truth of the testimony, and if it is found to be false, the witness can be prosecuted for perjury. See PERJURY.

THEFT. Taking another person's property with the intent to deprive the rightful owner.

TITLE.   The legal ownership of property, usually real property (such as land). It is often referred to as a deed.

TORT.   A injury or wrong committed on the person (his body) or property of another.

TRANSCRIPT.   A word-for-word typed record of everything that was said "on the record" during a trial. The court reporter types this transcription, which is paid for by the parties requesting it.

TRIAL COURT.   The court of original jurisdiction; the first court to consider the litigation (or legal action).

VENUE.   The proper geographical area, county, city, or district in which to bring a lawsuit.

VOIR DIRE.   A French phrase meaning to see and to speak. It is the process of questioning potential jurors so that the attorneys on both sides may decide whether to accept or oppose individuals to serve on the jury.

WAIVER.   The act of intentionally giving up a right.

WARRANT.   In most cases, a court order authorizing a law enforcement officer to make an arrest or conduct a search. See SEARCH WARRANT.

WITNESS.   One who testifies to what he or she has seen, heard, or otherwise experienced.

WRIT.   A judicial order directing a person to do or not do some specific act.

INDEX

NOTES

NOTES

NOTES

NOTES

NOTES

NOTES

NOTES

NOTES

NOTES

NOTES

NOTES

Also available, FACILITATOR'S GUIDE to **IT'S THE LAW!** $16.95
with instructional preface from author, expanded glossary and mock trial.

_____ × $12.95 = _____ It's The Law! A Young Person's Guide to Our
Legal System

_____ × $16.95 = _____ Facilitator's Guide to It's The Law!

add $4.50 Shipping & Handling $4.50 for first book,

_____ × $1.00 = _____ $1.00 each additional book.

_____ _California resident please add appropriate sales tax._

Total Enclosed: _____

Save more by ordering the following _postage paid_ packages.

Package 1: Includes 10 copies of It's The Law! A Young Person's Guide to
Our Legal System and 1 Facilitator's Guide to It's The Law!
Retail price: $146.45 **Discount Price: $124.95 postage paid**

Package 2: Includes 25 copies of It's The Law! A Young Person's Guide to
Our Legal System and 1 Facilitator's Guide to It's The Law!
Retail price: $340.70 **Discount Price: $267.95 postage paid**

Please send _____ Package 1 at $124.95 each for a total of $_____

Please send _____ Package 2 at $267.95 each for a total of $_____

Additional copies available at discount. Please call for prices.
1-800-879-9636 Fax: 209-296-4515

☐ Please send me your free complete catalogs.

Ship To:

Name/Attention _____

Company/School _____

Address _____

City _____ State _____ Zip _____

Daytime Phone # _____

Volcano Press
P.O. Box 270 YL
Volcano, CA 95689